THE TEENAGER AND THE NEW MORALITY

THE TEENAGER
AND
THE NEW MORALITY

ROBERT RAAB, D.H.L.

RICHARDS ROSEN PRESS, NEW YORK, N.Y. 10010

/70.202
R ///t

Standard Book Number: 8239–0218–8
Library of Congress Catalog Card Number: 74–116620

Published in 1970 by Richards Rosen Press, Inc.
29 East 21st Street, New York City, N.Y. 10010

Revised Edition

Manufactured in the United States of America

DEDICATION:

To my parents—Sam and Emma Raab—who brought me into
    the world—and have that special faith and love which
    parents reserve for a child.
To my dear wife Margie and sons Daniel and Joel—who helped
    so much, by just believing that I had something
    worthwhile to say.
To Ruth Rosen—gifted guide and wise counselor—who
    encouraged me to set down my thoughts in this book.
To the Teenager of today—who lives in a world of difficult
    choices and decisions.

Ben Zoma said: *Who is wise?* He who learns from
        all men.

                      (Sayings of the Fathers)

About the Author

DR. ROBERT A. RAAB has devoted much of his life's work to youth. While still a student, he was a member of the faculty of the first Leadership Institute for high-school youth, sponsored by the National Federation of Temple Youth. He has been the Dean of numerous Camp Conclaves and Leadership Institutes, and his Temple has pioneered the "weekend away at camp" program for the upper grades of the religious school. Much of the material in this book grew out of conversations that Dr. Raab has had with his teenage sons, Daniel and Joel. He feels that we must listen to the voices of our young people as we seek to guide them during the teenage years, and that this is especially true when viewing the problems raised by the "new" morality.

Dr. Raab received a B.A. degree from the University of Cincinnati, and was ordained at the Hebrew Union College–Jewish Institute of Religion, where he earned the degree of Doctor of Hebrew Letters. He has served as Rabbi of Temple B'nai Israel, in McKeesport, Pennsylvania, and is now Rabbi of the Suburban Temple in Wantagh, Long Island, New York. In addition to his duties as Rabbi, he also teaches in the Sociology Department of Nassau Community College. He is a past president of the Wantagh Clergy Council and of the Long Island Association of Reform Rabbis. He has also served on the Youth Committee and the Committee on Marriage and Family Life of the Central Conference of American Rabbis. He has written for such periodicals as *American Judaism,* the *Journal of the Central Conference of American Rabbis, The Jewish Spectator,* and *The Jewish Criterion.*

Dr. Raab is a native of Cleveland, Ohio. His wife, the former Marjorie Klein, of Hopkinsville, Kentucky, is a coordinating counselor of students at Nassau Community College.

7

Purpose

The purpose of this book is to show how teenagers are responding to what has been termed the new morality. What are the new standards and norms of conduct? Is there such a thing as morality and immorality? What criteria are applied by today's youth in evolving modes of conduct? Moral patterns are in flux. Young people are developing their own codes of behavior. Together we shall explore what may be termed the "morality explosion." War, violence, drugs, the Pill—these are the rubrics of the new age. Within a few years, the majority of the population will be under the age of 25. The moral style of today's teenager may give us a clue to the morality of tomorrow.

Contents

THE TEENAGER AND THE NEW MORALITY

The Search for Morality

A college student declares, "Someone who changes his beliefs is immoral, if it's a major change to fit situations. An aborigine who gets a new set of beliefs from a missionary is moral. He has found a new way of life. But he is immoral if he changes back to his old ways, once the missionary leaves. A moral person does not live by expediency."

His high-school-age brother chimes in, "A moral person is one who leads his life according to his own beliefs. There are no set criteria to determine morality. Unless someone infringes on your beliefs, he is entitled to his own beliefs. Yet, each man is not just an island to himself." I reply, "You belong to a generation that is fashioning its own code of moral behavior. You want consistency and an attitude that seems to say 'I can do my own thing, provided I do not hurt someone else.' Morality becomes a matter of individual judgment."

The foregoing discussion was with two youths who were confirmed at the temple I serve as Rabbi. Not once did they mention the Ten Commandments as a possible guide to conduct. I asked, "Does religion play a role in your life?" The reply was, "Very few high-school or college students think much of religious institutions. College freshmen tend to be cynical about the religious establishment. Organized religion has failed the young people. Youth today do have a religious 'feeling' but it has little to do with formal religious institutions."

Those are some of the realities that permeate your world. Many of your views are shared by adults. The question of what makes a moral person is extremely difficult. Earlier ages had definite answers. Morality derived from God or gods. The great religions of Western civilization evolved One-God faiths. God was a source of the moral order in the universe. Immanuel Kant, the philosopher, believed that God's rules were present everywhere. It was man's task to discover them. Then man could shape his life according to the moral rules laid down by the Deity.

Today, rules are promulgated, and small sects live by them. Often they are religious fundamentalists who accept the Bible literally and thus find in Scripture the source of inspiration and conduct. For most young people, the moral commitment arises elsewhere. The life-style of today has brought forth the term "the new morality."

"What do you think of the new morality?" I asked my 13-year-old son. "What is the new morality? What do you think I'm talking about?"

"Oh, you mean free love," he said with a quick smile.

The youth entering his teens is already aware, even if vaguely, of the question of morality. An ancient religious maxim declares: "Train up a child in the way, and he will walk therein." Morality involves much more than free love. It has to do with how you react to a given situation. In a pragmatic sense, what we are—and how we act—is determined by the values learned at the family hearth.

Your Family

"The Youth Communes—New Way of Living Confronts the U.S." Those words herald the cover story in a popular weekly magazine.[1] The location of the commune is not revealed. It is populated by "dropouts" from the mainstream of American life. The forty-one-member commune calls itself a "family." They are all part of the same family group. Everything is shared. The majority have fled from the cities to create a new life-style, on the land. The local inhabitants are hostile. The commune is peopled by young adults—mostly under 30—with young children.

It is a free and open society in which each works hard to wrest a living from the earth. The commune-dwellers are deeply religious. They pray and fast. Said one: "We chose to devote our lives to God and the lessons He teaches in the earth." [2] Their credo: "Getting out of the cities isn't hard, only concrete is. Get it together. This means on your own, all alone or with a few of your friends. Buy land. Don't rent. Money manifests. Trust. Plant a garden. Create a center. Come together." [3]

The new hippie commune life-style has been tried before in America. In 1848 the Oneida Community was founded by John Humphrey Noyes. A system of "complex marriage" was instituted, in which all men and all women were to love one another. Children were raised in separate quarters, apart from their parents. By 1880 the community was dissolved. Outside pressures and internal dissent led to the demise of the experiment.

The Soviets experimented with the family structure after the Bolshevik revolution. Children were taught that their first loyalty was to the state. The family was attacked as the source of counter-revolutionary sentiments and corrupt capitalistic ways. Children were encouraged to spy on their parents. By 1936 the Soviets had reversed that policy. The family was restored to its central role. Antimarriage sentiments were reversed. Divorce laws became more strict. The attempt at communal socialistic-style life was lost.

The most successful experiment in group living has been carried on in Israel, where some 80,000 people live on collective farms called *kibbutzim*. In Israel a few years ago, I visited a *kibbutz* populated by North Americans. The children were raised in separate dormitories and saw their parents only in the morning and evening. When I spoke with them, the parents seemed satisfied with the arrangements. "I see my children at the end of the day when I can play with them, without distraction. The children do not suffer. They are healthy and active."

The *kibbutzim* are collective farms. The earliest of them, founded a generation or more ago, were the initial effort to reclaim the land of Palestine. Formal marriage was rare. Yet the common-law-style marriages were binding. Although the "arrangement" was not sanctified by the clergy, strong group pressure operated to prevent its dissolution. The new generation born on the *kibbutzim* are now requesting marriage by a rabbi. In some cases, they are urging their parents to get married! The new morality on the *kibbutz* is a return to an older, more conventional approach to marriage. Fewer *kibbutzim* are being formed today in Israel. Instead, they have the *moshav*, a village where families live in individual homes, communally share their farm implements, and support a common shopping, recreation, and school area.

History indicates that "off-beat" experiments in group living either do not survive or are gradually modified to conform to more conventional patterns of behavior.

As a teenager, chances are you are growing up in a family that consists of yourself, your parents, and another child or two. What you are will be greatly influenced by what you see and hear at home. A social philosopher named Marshall McLuhan has said, "The medium is the message." What you are, as a person, is what you project toward others. The home is the "medium" that molds you. The "message" is what you do as a result of what you learn within the family circle. You project yourself into the larger world while carrying within you your home-formed values.

In our homes, a moral climate is created. "Morality" means knowing right from wrong. For example, at the dinner table a father says, "Well, it's income tax time again. I've got a smart new accountant who says he will show me some new ways to beat Uncle Sam. The government expects you to cheat a little. Besides, the government takes too much anyway. Most of our tax dollars are wasted. Look at the bureaucracy in Washington, with its waste and duplication. Government is largely a fraud. The less we send them, the less they will squander. They even encourage cheating. Every taxpayer is allowed an automatic 10 percent deduction for contributions to charity. How many actually give that much?"

Some see nothing wrong in cheating the phone company. Mother says: "When your plane lands, call collect from the airport. Ask for yourself. I will not accept the charges, but I will know you arrived safe and sound." The philosophy is: "What's wrong with a free phone call? The phone company makes plenty on us. Especially with two teenagers in our house!"

It is difficult for you to correct your parents. It is not easy to challenge their moral attitudes or pretensions. What you see and hear, you are likely to absorb. You also may imitate their actions. Much has been said and written about the American home. As a teenager you will spend most of your time in contact with your family. The things you see will affect and shape your personality. How will you react to your home situation? I read about a young man who was highly critical of his friends when they would take a drink. He was very demanding of his peers. He was considered unusually "straitlaced"; he reacted violently to any deviation from model behavior. He did not drink or smoke. He upbraided those who did. It was learned that he came from a family in which the father was a drunkard who abandoned him and his mother when he was an infant. The young man was overreacting to his father's weakness and infidelity. Having had a difficult childhood, he was rigid and unbending in the matter of conduct. He carried the scars of yesterday with him. Secretly he may have feared that his father's weakness for alcohol might one day take hold of him. A person who overreacts and constantly moralizes about actions that are not inherently evil may himself have serious emotional problems.

What we are derives from heredity (what we inherit biologically) and from environment (the people around us).

"Our youth now love luxury. They have bad manners, contempt for authority, disrespect for older people. Children nowadays are tyrants. They no longer rise when their elders enter the room. They contradict their parents, chatter before company, gobble their food and tyrannize their teachers." The above complaints are not new. They were spoken by Socrates before 400 B.C. Actually, there is reason to believe that Socrates cribbed the whole thing, since travelers can see the identical passage on an ancient papyrus in a museum in Istanbul.[4]

Socrates blamed the youth. Parental disappointment and disapproval of young people goes back further than Socrates. In the Bible, one of Noah's sons is punished because he fails to cover his father's nakedness when he (Noah) is in a drunken stupor. Noah curses his son Ham and tells him he will be a "servant of servants to his brothers" for his failure to act decently (Genesis 9:18–28). Noah overreacted. He blamed his son for not coming to his aid. He said not a word about his own drunken condition.

In a TV drama, a father confronts his son who has been arrested for selling drugs to other high-school students. "Why did you do this?" the father cries out in anguish. "Didn't we raise you in a nice home and give you every advantage?"

The boy replies, "What makes you act so self-righteously? Who do you think you were kidding when you cheated on Mom? We saw you more than once go into a hotel with your secretary during what was supposed to be an 'afternoon business conference.' " The father was crushed by his son's accusations. He could not answer. "Do as I say, not as I do" seldom produces desired results. Often a child cannot forgive his parents for wrongdoing. What you see your parents do can have a tremendous effect on you.

Sociologists use the term "nuclear" to describe the typical American family. This means a small family unit, consisting of the parents and usually two or three children. Because the family is small, emotional reactions are intense, since they are limited to the few. In an earlier age, when large families were in vogue, a teenager could find stabilizing forces with a large variety of aunts, uncles, cousins, and grandparents. In rural America, two or possibly three generations would live under one roof. If a parent were away, a grandmother was always nearby who had ample time to listen to you pour out your complaints, desires, or confusions. Today, that is not the case. When you come home from school, bursting with an exciting event to discuss, Mother may be at a bridge game, or still at work. The nuclear family often has two working parents. Togetherness in the home can be severely limited.

A distraught mother rushed into my study and cried, "What should I do, Rabbi? My teenage son constantly berates me because I have a full-time job. Our family needs the money. I simply have to work to make ends meet. He complains I'm never home."

A few minutes after she left my office, another mother rushed in. "Rabbi, I'm very upset. My daughter needles me all the time for just staying home. She has been urging me to get a job, so as to do something useful. Nothing I do or say pleases her." Parents cannot win!

Parents are confused. They wish to provide you with all the necessities and good things that life has to offer. To do so, many mothers are in the work force. More than 30 percent of the married women in the United States have full or part-time jobs. Is it morally right for a mother to be employed? College education for her child is not free. Clothes must be bought. Vacations are pleasant. Money is very useful. Still, you should also be aware that some mothers work because they really enjoy being out in the world. Housework is drudgery. They can be better mothers simply because they are doing something enjoyable and satisfying to themselves.

Even as you are concerned with your personal happiness and fulfillment, so, too, is your mother. Some women are quite content to be at home. No two parents are exactly alike, even as no two teenagers are exactly alike. What pleases you may be very distasteful to your friend. To recognize that a parent has needs is a mark of maturity.

How do you react to your home situation? If a parent is authoritarian and rigid, children learn to act accordingly. If a parent is permissive, the child will adjust. Some psychologists say that the worst problems arise as a result of a lack of consistency.

The father who is kind and loving one day and flies into an uncontrollable rage the next only confuses the family. You need to know what to expect; then you can regulate your conduct accordingly.

You are influenced by your home. Parents who overindulge their children with gifts may find that the children spend recklessly when they grow up. On the other hand are those parents who squander the family funds on themselves, leaving little for the children. Such youngsters can develop deep-seated resentment against their parents.

The Ideal Family

Let us construct the perfect family. The father is always cheerful and interested in his wife and children. The children greet the father with a warm "hello" as he comes home from a hard day's work at the office. The mother is beautifully dressed as she places the dinner on the table. Ever the gracious hostess, the mother is not annoyed when baby brother spills the milk. "I will wipe it up for you, darling," she says with a sweet smile. Father laughs indulgently at the antics of Junior, who has just kicked his younger sister Betsy under the table. Betsy laughs and says, "Junior, you are such a tease!" Life is calm and sweet. Nobody is overly disturbed. All runs smoothly.

Have we been describing the ideal family? Certainly not. The family that does not move from crisis to crisis is rare. Each person within your family unit is an individual—possessed of feelings and emotions. A family without anger, hostility, and friction can exist only in a cardboard cutout. Dissent and difference of opinion are the essence of life. Living would be dull if we were all one-dimensional robots. You can program a computer. You cannot program a person. Brothers do quarrel and fight. If father has a bad day at work, he may take it out on the wife and children. If mother has had a bad day, with everything going wrong, she is likely to be in an edgy mood come evening. If a child has done poorly on a test, he may vent his anger on a younger brother or sister. A family is much like a ship at sea. At times, there is calm sailing; other times, storms arise. A ship is seaworthy in relationship to its ability to ride out the storm. Similarly, a family goes through storm and stress. The strength of the family is found in its ability to survive the difficult times, so as to regain balance and purpose.

You come to see that parents are human. When angry, they may use foul language. They say things that they will later regret. They may say, "I'm sorry I spoke as I did. You were upset, and so was I. Let's talk things over." At that point, you should be willing to accept their apology and listen to them.

What do you hope your parents will do when you have a problem? They should listen to you. Blessed is the family with a teenager who feels free to sit down with mom and dad to discuss an urgent matter. A sympathetic, listening ear is much to be desired.

"I can talk to my mother. She really cares. She understands. She was young once. We do not always agree. But even if she says 'no,' at least she tries to give me a reason for her decision." Morality is caught, even more than it is taught. As a rabbi, I have discovered that preaching an ethical message means little, unless the congregant is ready to listen and really wants to develop a better approach to life. You can help create a better situation in your own home if you do not look for perfection in others. Mothers are not always in the mood to talk to you, even as you at times wish privacy and silence.

What can you do? Do not turn a deaf ear to your parents' words; you may discover that your parents are wiser than you think. Mark Twain said it was amazing how much smarter his parents became in his eyes as he grew older. You will someday share the same world and many of the same problems with your parents. Their views are worth hearing, even if you disagree.

The Family of the Future?

Albert Rosenfeld has written a book called *The Second Genesis* in which he theorizes that "Radical new techniques in biology promise (or threaten) a near future world of reproduction that is artificially assisted or even sexless and of babies grown in glass wombs in the laboratory. The new facts of life raise questions about the attitudes people have toward science, sex, and tomorrow's morality." [5] He holds that we may see the end of the institutions of marriage and the family when the biological revolution takes place. How will parents feel toward test-tube babies? How would you feel toward your mother, if you were a test-tube child? Those are only hypothetical questions for most youths and their parents. Traditionally, the child is the product of the marriage bed. If that situation changes, the family may be altered in a radical way.

Almost since the dawn of time, the family has existed. It has survived wars, famine, disease, and dislocation. It will survive the new biology, but the form may be altered. Even as an adopted child is dearly loved, so will the parents come to love their test-tube offspring.

A respondent to a Lou Harris poll on the "new reproduction" declared, "When you hold a baby who depends on you in your arms, you don't worry about where the egg came from." [6]

Our Friends

You are influenced by the crowd. But at school you find a number of diverse crowds. You can often find the group that shares your ideas and ideals. Or, if such a group does not exist, you can form one yourself. Does your community have a Young Dems or a Young Republicans club? You would be surprised how quickly political leaders will gladly sponsor or help you organize such a group. The accent today is on youth. The candidate who fires the imagination of the young people is the one who will win office—if not today, then tomorrow. Within a few years, more than 50 percent of the population will be under the age of 25. Political leaders are cultivating the voters of the future. You are in that favored category.

"I don't have any new friends. I'm always with the same crowd." Sometimes you think or say that. Ways can be found to meet and make new friends. Your church or synagogue probably has a young people's group. There are socials, dances, discussion, and, yes—creative services. Ministers are aware that religion must change. From the altar of the synagogue or church you will hear the guitars and the voices of youth. The rock or folk-music service has even become a standard part of the ritual in some houses of worship.

One temple has a "coffee-house" service on Friday evenings. The youths gather in a part of the temple basement that has been converted into a "coffee house," complete with checkered table-cloths, amplifiers, a small stage, and candles furnishing soft light. Spontaneous services are held, as well as impromptu musical programs. The teenagers bring their own musical instruments. It is informal and casual. The rabbi in charge of the program reports that some of the youngsters drift upstairs to use the temple library. Instead of the corner candy store, we now have the coffee house in the temple. My own congregation has set aside a youth lounge, complete with jukebox, pool tables, and Ping-Pong facilities. Here, the youth group meets for services, dances, parties, and cultural discussions. The "study supper" with the rabbi is a regular event.

The boy or girl who is active in his church or temple group is no longer considered "square." Becoming active in a religious youth group has certain advantages. You make new friends in an atmosphere that has parental approval. Your parents know where you are. The activities often can be—and are—fun.

It is natural to want to be a part of the crowd. The question is, which crowd? A youth comments: "I used to go only with the kids at my school. In the Temple Youth group, I met a swell bunch of kids from another school. It is nice to meet new boys and girls. At youth camp we met kids from all over the state. One of them is going to visit me over Thanksgiving. Sure, services are nice at religious youth camp. But it's meeting people you never knew—that's the real value!" To be part of a group is to find fulfillment. Much of your moral conduct will be influenced by your friends.

Is it possible to harmonize what the "gang" does with what parents demand or desire? One way is to talk things over with the leader of your group. Do not remain silent. If the gang wishes to act in a way that is contrary to your best judgment or instinct, it is possible to say "no." A thoughtful young man remarked: "My friends found an abandoned house. Each night they threw rocks through the windows. It was great sport, so they said. I was invited to join them in their activities. I said 'no.' They were picked up by the police one night. I was glad not to be a part of that adventure."

The ability to say "no" to your friends is also a mark of maturity. A mature teenager said: "The kids I used to hang around with began to change. The boys decided it would be fun to 'have fun' with a girl who had a reputation for 'putting out.' It somehow went against me to do this. Gradually I found that I was not included in their activities. I made new friends, who felt more as I did. It wasn't easy at first. Now, I'm glad I did what I did." To buck the crowd and set your own standards is difficult. But it can be done if you want to "do your own thing" according to your own taste and judgment.

Philosophers now speak of "existential" reality. The existentialist is trying to discover why he exists and what—if any—purpose there is to life. Some existentialists tend to be gloomy about the future. They feel that all is lost. The world is going to ruin. Nothing can stop the drift. Some campus radicals fall into that trap. They say, "We must tear down the Establishment, or it will destroy us. Down with all conventions. Down with all moral values." Such a philosophy does have a limited appeal. In "telling it like it is," the pessimist can see only the dark side of life. He is without hope. Youth is a time when feelings and desires fluctuate. One day you feel on top of the world; the next day, something can happen to plunge you into the darkest gloom. Maturity involves a balancing of the forces at work inside—and outside— of ourselves. The existentialist is right when he says, "Man exists." The problem is: How do we discover the moral values that shape our lives?

CHAPTER II

Identity and Dissent

We do live, at least in part, by certain models. The long-hair craze may have started with the Beatles, was picked up by the teen and college crowd, and ended up with the Madison Avenue executive. Sideburns and long hair are not restricted to the "hip" group. People of all ages latched onto the hair and sideburns fad.

The young have heroes. The soldier is not the hero in our age. The political leader who brings the troops home is admired. The young people today seem to search for heroes of their own age. Perhaps you have become disillusioned with the hypocrisy and sham found in the adult world. You seem to be saying, "Since adults are not with it for civil rights and peace, we will have to do it ourselves."

A previous generation screamed when Frank Sinatra appeared. Your parents look back with nostalgia to the age of swing, when Benny Goodman, Harry James, and others set the pace. Boogie-woogie was in. Today it is rock and "soul" that capture many young people. As a teenager you seek to discover your own identity. In so doing, it is natural for you to be influenced by your peers—those of your generation.

You share secrets, dreams, and thoughts with your friends. You simply cannot share everything with your parents. Adults do not know the names of the latest hit recording group. They may still think that the "Brooklyn Bridge" is a physical structure. They have seen "stone ponies" in the park with generals perched on them. They have never awakened to or tasted a "strawberry alarm clock." Fads come and go. Soul music may turn you on

28

and turn your parents off. The blast of the stereo and the beat you find so attractive may drive them to distraction. Yet the music they play may also be a bore or annoyance to you.

In life we live with conflict. That is not always bad. If we all thought alike, we would end up in a world with the "bland leading the bland." Sameness is deadly. That is why overweight people go off their diets. Too much cottage cheese and eggs creates monotony. Life demands variety. Were parents to agree to everything the "gang" decides, then all authority would crumble, and anarchy would hold sway. Some psychologists feel that youth really does want to know what the limitations of approved conduct are.

Discussion and negotiated settlement between the generations is often the answer when difficulties arise. "My parents say I must be in by midnight on Saturday evening. The school dance is over at twelve. I discussed this with them. They were willing to relax the curfew until one, so that I could get my date home— and even have time for a brief late snack with the gang. My folks were understanding. They are willing to bend the rules, when I can show them good reason for doing so."

Our Schools

Many teenagers say they dislike school. Yet most of their conversation is about school, curriculum, and teachers. The teachers are analyzed and discussed constantly. Certain ones are rated as "terrific." Others are considered a "drag" or worse. "Miss Smith wears her skirts too short. Sure, she's a young teacher, but why does she feel she has to act so sexy?"

"Mr. Jones is a dope. He can't control his class. Unless I sit in the front row, I can't hear anything. He can't teach us because he permits so much noise."

"Mr. Corwin is a bag of wind. It's easy to get him off the subject. You can tell he is only interested in the sound of his own voice."

"Miss Hayes is really great. All the kids like her. She doesn't mind staying after school to explain things. She is the first to volunteer to help the committee for the class prom. You know she really likes us."

No two teachers are alike. You are influenced by each one, for good or bad. An excellent history teacher may point you in the direction of becoming an historian. A poor science teacher may turn you away from that field, even if you had a real interest in it. Teachers are a moral guide and example, whether or not they want to be: "Everyone cheats on tests. Mr. Worthman pretends he doesn't see what is going on. He wants to be everyone's friend. He wants to be liked. But he makes it hard for the kids who studied and who resent cheaters. Why doesn't he stop them?"

The following situation arises: You are taking a final exam. Suddenly you panic. Your mind goes blank. Your neighbor's paper is in view. He seems to have the correct answers. Should you copy from him? Can you get away with it? What if you get caught? You need a high grade even to pass the course. Your ultimate decision on whether to cheat will be shaped by a number of considerations. You can cheat on the test, then rationalize as to why you did so. ("Rationalization" means making an excuse for acting in a certain way.) You can excuse yourself by thinking, "The test was unfair. The teacher did not adequately review the material. Not enough time was allowed for this test. A good teacher would have really taught us the material. I never was any good in this subject." All of us rationalize at some time or another. It is far easier to duck the issue than to face our own inadequacies. I recall a TV celebrity who was commenting on the question of cheating. She said, "I would hate to be operated on by a surgeon who cheated his way through medical school!"

You might argue that your life is not at stake when the temptation exists to cheat on a test. You are in no physical danger, to be sure. But what of your mental and emotional reactions? How will you feel after you turn in the paper, when you have copied someone else's work? Religionists would argue that your conscience might bother you. Your friends may say, "Everyone cheats. Why be left out? Your grades will suffer if you are honest."

Once at the seminary I attended, a student brought an English Bible to class. He used it to help him translate passages from Hebrew that were on the test. When the instructor came in the room, the boy quickly threw the Bible out of the window, to hide his act. The young man was ordained, but left the ministry after a few years.

When faced with the opportunity to cheat, you may simply decide not to copy from your neighbor. Many a student has learned from sad experience that it is possible to copy the wrong answers. You may be better prepared than the person seated near you. The consequences of cheating can be severe. You may decide it is foolish to risk failing a course just to get an answer. Cheaters have been apprehended. The embarrassment may not be worth the risk. Instead of rationalizing, your ultimate choice can be just to do your best.

You may feel that the question is a matter of moral judgment. If cheating is wrong, why do it? External and internal consequences can be painful. Why risk facing parents, teachers, and friends with a possible black mark on your record?

To cheat or not to cheat—that is the question. "Thou shalt not steal" is a Biblical Commandment. Legal action is taken when one firm steals an invention from another firm. The patent system is designed to protect the inventor from those who would steal the fruits of his genius. Penalties exist for those who copy the works of others. A religious fundamentalist might, in a literal sense, consider stealing answers a mortal sin. Even if considered a minor sin, it can be troublesome to the conscience.

A college student summed it up this way: "Cheating is immoral because it does hurt others in the class who have studied for the exam. Their grades will be affected if the cheaters are not caught. If everyone gets a high mark, the teacher may then grade the exam on a curve. The noncheater is thus cheated."

Other situations can be aggravating. "In our school, the homework assignments are supposed to be staggered. Yet the teachers don't care. Some weeks we have very little to do. Other weeks we are loaded down with homework. Why don't the teachers follow the school policy?"

"I stayed out from school on a religious holiday. The teacher gave a major test. Now I have to take a make-up. It just isn't fair."

Teenagers cannot always effect change. Some fear that the teachers will punish them if they speak up. The teacher's favor is still important, even in this age of student unrest and protest. "He is still the one to give me my final mark. Why should I look for trouble?"

"We were told that we had to turn in our notebooks by a certain date. It was implied that our grades would be affected by the neatness of the notebook. I spent two full days typing up my notes. Then the teacher decided not to collect them. I handed her the notebook and said, 'Here it is. I worked hard on it.' Isn't it immoral of a teacher not to collect them, when she made this required work?"

"The last week of school we were suddenly told we were responsible for the material in the last five chapters of our history book, even though we had not gotten to the material in class discussion. Is it fair to be tested on material you have not covered?" A pupil should not be held responsible for the teacher's lack of organization of her teaching time.

"My teacher makes me mad. She asks us to do homework, and it is not collected or graded." When teachers are unfair, you should bring the matter up at your student government meetings. When adults have meetings, there is usually time at the end for "good and welfare." Such should also be the procedure within the school system.

A student remarked: "In our school the principal objected to the way some of the girls were dressed. They tried to work out a dress code. Students and teachers formed a committee to handle the problem. Finally the whole idea of a dress code was abandoned. It was just too hard to set standards. Styles are changing too rapidly. If a boy or girl is really dressed in a truly outlandish or offensive way, the principal will send the offender home to change. That's about all he could do."

A principal once told me the following: "A certain girl in the Junior High insisted on wearing skin-tight blouses and mini-skirts that were just too revealing. I called the mother in to discuss the problem. When she walked in, I could see it was a lost cause. The mother's blouse was even tighter than the daughter's! Her skirt was even shorter—if it's possible—than that of her offspring. What could I do? How can you discipline such a parent?"

Where Do We Go From Here?

School administrators do not work in a vacuum. They must be responsive to the needs and wishes of the community. Parents are vocal. School boards tend to shape decisions to fit community requests. I have been at meetings of our local school board that were attended by teenagers. Very often they will speak out on matters of major concern. The P.T.A. is another place to speak out. On one occasion a delegation of young people came to a P.T.A. meeting to demand better recreational facilities for youth. One of them said: "There is no place to go on Saturday night. If we are walking the sidewalks after ten, then the police cars stop us for loitering. How about opening the schools on Saturday nights for a Teen Canteen-type program?"

"The key to what is going on among high-school students today," Louis Harris reports, "is that a majority clearly want to participate more in deciding their future. They are willing to be taught, but not to be told. They are willing to abide by rules, but they will not abide by rules which put them down. They are aware of the need for authority, but not impressed by it for its own sake. They are excited by the prospect of living in a fast-changing modern society and they want their high-school education to help prepare them for it—not for some society of the past." [7] A Harris poll taken at Woodward High in Cincinnati revealed that 66 percent of the students wanted a role in determining school rules and curriculum. More than half of them felt they should have a say in setting up discipline, as well as having a voice in the way classes would be conducted. The poll revealed that teachers, principals, and parents were in strong opposition to greater student participation in decision-making areas.

Harris did find some areas of agreement. Students, parents, and teachers felt that in-class discussion of drug use should take place. Also, "41 percent of the parents joined 52 percent of the students and 62 percent of the teachers in encouraging sex education. But when it came to black students' rights, underground papers and movies, hair and dress styles, and folkrock music, both teachers and parents parted company with the young." [8] It is obvious from the Harris survey that more than half of today's high-school students are impatient and filled with discontent over the limited participation they have in shaping the policies that govern their education.

The militant feeling found in high schools has also been reflected on the college campus. A July 1969 Harris survey of 1,005 seniors in fifty colleges and universities reveals that 72 percent of them are sympathetic to the campus militants. Some 63 percent of the students felt there was no need to strengthen U.S. military defenses in the world. On the other hand, the general adult population favored such strengthening by 54 to 33 percent.

> The keys to student thinking today from this survey are that they are deeply convinced that the United States "should not engage in military ventures such as Vietnam again," that those who violate the peace "should be dealt with through international machinery, such as the U.N. or a combination of allies," and that the main concentration of activity in our national life should be on domestic issues such as combating discrimination against blacks and other minorities, helping the poor, and rectifying injustices wherever they exist. Perhaps, most of all, the students want to begin on their own campuses by exercising "student power" in decisions over curriculum, faculty appointments, admissions, and other areas traditionally reserved for administration and faculty handling and control.[9]

Harris further noted that the students were incensed by the "hypocrisy of the establishment." He went on to say:

> They see far more hypocrisy in establishment types such as an embezzling bank president than in a bank robber, in an immoral businessman than in a long-haired hippie, in a white grocer who sells his Negro customers bad meat than in a black rioter.[10]

The Harris survey shows that youth is setting its own moral standards. Young people want honesty and decency now. If schools reflect the hypocrisy of the general society, then they will continue to be under fire. Law-and-order repression on the campus can only alienate the young people of our land.

Authority figures—be they principals, deans, teachers, or parents, will receive respect only when they deserve it. My generation did little complaining. We went to school to receive an education and were willing to endure boring teachers and poor curricula. Many of today's adults are products of the immigrant generation. Our parents sacrificed so that we could attain a college degree. Money was scarce. You did not dare be too vocal. The immigrant, who had difficulty mastering English, as well as the American mores, was not in the mood to tolerate insubordination. The teacher was like God. She could not be questioned.

Such is no longer the case. Parents listen. If the child has a valid complaint, the parent is likely to call the principal. The following is a typical comment: "At our dinner table, Mom asks me about my teachers. She is highly critical of those teachers who cannot control our classes—or who are goofing off and too lazy to teach. I have one teacher who does nothing but pass out ditto sheets every day. Is this teaching? She tells us to learn the material by ourselves. Another teaches by showing movies every day. The kid who operates the projector gets the best grade."

Parents do react to what you have to say. The time is past when the teacher's word was law. Reverence for the schoolteacher is now replaced by critical probing. There is less tolerance for poor teaching. Not every complaint by a student is justified. Still, I believe that much of your criticism is valid enough to warrant investigation.

Technology and Hypocrisy

America has the technology to put men on the moon. We have been able to move ahead in the conquest of outer space. With all of the promise of American genius, many of our teenagers—and a majority of college-age young people—are disillusioned with the promise of tomorrow. What should be a grand period of opening up to the possibilities of the future has turned to sour grapes. Gloom and disillusionment are found at every turn.

Some feel that youth is overwhelmed by the enormity of the world and its many problems. At the multiversity with 40,000 other students, he finds his name on an IBM card. His grades are sent to him by code number. He watches lectures on TV monitors at the back of a huge hall. It is no wonder that the Berkeley uprising of 1964 took place. What began as the free-speech movement on that campus soon spread to campuses throughout America. The Berkeley incident began with what now appears to have been a modest request for a microphone and political recruiting tables in Sproul Plaza. Sit-ins and confrontations with authorities soon followed. Opposition to R.O.T.C. was voiced. From many campuses came the demand to end the war in Vietnam and the draft. The screaming student was saying, "Here I am. Listen to me. I am a person. There is much that is immoral. There is much that has to be changed."

Columbia was one of the universities to be embroiled in conflict. When the original list of six demands was presented, "an SDS leader was asked what the group would do if all six demands were accepted. He replied: make six more demands. The tactic of constant pressure is an old revolutionary strategy: the object is not reform but to bring down the 'corrupt' society." [11]

Campus rebels fall into two categories: those who wish to tear down the Establishment, and those who wish to change the Establishment. Each group has one thing in common: They are not happy with things the way they are. They want to be considered as much more than a number on an IBM card. Radical change can only destroy. The campus anarchist who denies free speech to others, while claiming the right of free speech for himself, is practicing hypocrisy.

After an S.D.S. speaker forced his way to the microphone at the 1969 Harvard graduation exercises, "the regular student speaker arose, a law graduate named Meldon Levine. The voice of the moderate majority was heard. . . . 'For attempting to achieve the values which you have taught us to cherish, your response has been astounding. It has escalated from the presence of police on the campuses to their use of clubs and gas. I have asked many of my classmates what they wanted me to say today. "Talk with them about hypocrisy," most of them said. "Tell them they have broken the best heads in the country. . . . Tell them they have destroyed our confidence and lost our respect." ' " [12]

I do not believe that all is lost in the relationship between the generations. A story is told of a young man who participated in the Columbia uprising of 1968. He was one of those occupying a building. Each day he called his worried parents to let them know he was all right. They pleaded with him to come home. He refused. Finally one morning his mother appeared at the school. "Son, I've brought you some chicken." The youth was embarrassed: "Aw, Ma, you shouldn't have done that. Besides, as part of the revolution we all share everything we have." The mother replied, "It's all right, son. I brought enough chicken for your friends, too!" This mother, of immigrant stock, did not fully understand the actions of her son. She responded to the problem in the only way she could. She brought him food. It was her way of saying, "I love you, son, even if I do not understand you."

What will the future hold for us? Only time will tell. The young are direct and vocal. Some feel that the "radicalization" of society is the only answer. Mark Rudd, student leader of the Columbia revolt, declared: "Confrontation politics puts the enemy up against the wall and forces him to define himself. In addition, it puts the individual up against the wall. He has to make a choice. Radicalization of the individual means that he must commit himself to the struggle to change society as well as share the radical view of what is wrong with society." [13]

Words such as "radicalization" and "confrontation" have become common. Seldom do we speak of gradual change or moderation. Youth is impatient, as it has always been. Adults are less likely to move quickly. Overstated demands have produced results. Those who wish to restructure the university have become convinced that just asking, pleading, and petitioning are not enough. When a worried college administration becomes fearful of a bad public image as the result of campus disorder, reforms quickly follow. Only the dramatic or unusual action commands the TV cameras.

You are part of the age of student dissent. You do not have a fixed definition of the word "morality." Young people equate morality with the freedom to do their own thing so long as no one else gets hurt. Unfortunately, that cannot always be so. What each person does has an effect on others. It is like dropping a stone into a quiet lake. The ripples move out in all directions. Your actions count. They affect others, be they parents, teachers, or friends. It is true that "No man is an island. No man stands alone." When we speak of morality, be it old or new, it does concern itself with how you act.

Your generation has a wonderful sense of openness to the new and the challenging. Youth remains potentially idealistic despite all of the problems of today. Your behavior is largely governed by your needs. You have a need to cry out against injustice. Yours is a concerned generation. Campus life—be it in high school or college—goes beyond fraternal and social organizations. I do not discount having fun. Yet more and more of your compatriots are aligning themselves with the concerned group that speaks for change.

With all its faults, American democracy allows for the greatest measure of dissent. Few other countries would permit the campus excesses of recent years. Even the Black Panthers who visited Cuba's "socialist paradise" were disillusioned to find that only Castro's brand of revolution was tolerated. If you demand the right to speak, you cannot deny the same right to others.

Morality involves decision-making. The *new* morality concerns itself with how you see the world, and how you react to its problems. An astronaut looking at the world from outer space sees a tiny ball floating in the vastness of the universe. He is aware that man can turn the earth into a place fully as barren of life as the moon. Man can foul the air and pollute the streams. He can destroy the forests and dump garbage into the rivers. He can produce enough poison gas to wipe out all life. He can press a button to release an atomic bomb. Man has the power to erase all earthly life. Your generation would adjudge that immoral. If morality involves individual actions that do or do not hurt others, then those who assault nature must be curbed.

In the book of Genesis is the story of Jacob's ladder. The base of it was on the earth. The top of it reached toward the heavens. The ladder symbolizes the human condition. We are "of this earth," yet—like the top of the ladder—we reach toward the stars. Religionists would say that man is at the same time both human and divine. His humanity is rooted in the earth and its concerns. Yet his idealism causes him to look upward to the stars.

As man flies to the moon, we may be moving into the post-industrial age. It takes a mechanical device to lift us out of earth's gravitational pull in order to fly toward the stars. It requires the genius of man to pilot his spacecraft to reach the moon and return in safety. It is man who controls the ship. It is man who

performs the corrections in navigation when the automatic devices fail. It is man who must exert control over the machine.
The terrifying scene in the film *2001: A Space Odyssey* occurs
when Hal, the computer, takes the control of the spacecraft
from the astronaut.

The college student who refuses to become a number on an
IBM card is in revolt against the computer. He demands the
right to be more than a figure on a tape. He is a person with
a name, feelings, desires, and a voice. He is not a robot who
responds to commands.

The great moral concern of the space age may be the entire
question of the purpose of our conquest of the stars. The tech-
nicians propel us to the moon. The poets and philosophers will
come later to tell us what it all really means. The moral danger may lie in whether the voice of the poet and the prophet
will be heard. To get a man to the moon requires that everything be carefully programmed and monitored. Spacemen do
have a sense of humor; but their task is a serious one. They
fly in a complex mechanical gadget. It is the end product of
today's technology and research. Over $23,000,000,000 was
expended to put man into lunar orbit and take him to the point
of stepping out onto the bare surface of that cold and burned-
out star.

Your generation (along with many adults) is now asking:
"Is it worth it?" Is it "obscene" to spend billions on rocketry
to race to the moon when we have riots and bloodshed in the
slums of our city? Urban decay goes largely unchecked. The
"other America" of which Michael Harrington speaks exists in
all of its ugliness. The urban and rural poor still live marginal
lives. The ghetto minorities still clamor for jobs, education, and
equal opportunity. The sensitive youth wonders at the folly of a
nation that neglects its own children while spending billions for
space research and armaments and war. Moral hypocrisy and
spiritual bankruptcy are ever present to the discerning eye. Only
the callous can look at the slums and then walk on, unconcerned.
Morality means to be concerned. It means that you *care*.

Affluence Is Not Enough

Even the most attractive and inviting suburban area does not guarantee morality. "You have to live in Scarsdale to know how bad it is." Those are the words of a youthful resident of that comfortable suburb. When the young turn their backs on affluence, parents are confused. They wonder, "How can this be? I have given my child every advantage. Where have I failed?"

The thinking young person is looking beyond affluence. Making money is only one goal. He or she wants to feel that there is more to life than a job. Life must be a fascinating challenge, full of hope and promise. Youth has always wanted that. Youth's new morality demands attention to both personal concerns (Who and what am I?) and external concerns (How can I make the planet livable again?).

The quest of youth for a new approach is apparent. Science with a heart is fine. Science that builds and does not destroy— that is what life is all about.

CHAPTER III

Sex and Love

I sat chatting with a close friend who is a physician. I asked, "Do you think moral standards are changing?"

He replied: "This year I have seen a sudden upsurge in unwed pregnant girls. Whereas in previous years perhaps one or two came into the office, this year I have seen at least eleven or twelve cases. One young lady came to the office with her boy friend. She was 21 and he was 24. He insisted that his girl friend was a virgin, and was shocked to hear she was pregnant. They had been keeping company for two years. His ignorance of sex was amazing. I asked each if they loved the other. They said they did. I suggested they get married quickly. They did. Sometimes a doctor has to be a marriage counselor." He added the last remark with a twinkle in his eye.

I continued, "How do you account for the new attitude?"

He went on: "Many unwed mothers feel no shame in being pregnant. Some are concerned about what their parents will say. Often they are confused. Some mothers discourage their daughters from using the birth control pills while at college— even though the girls ask for them. This is foolish on the mother's part. If her daughter becomes pregnant, it will be much worse."

The conversation drifted into the topic of abortion. The physician went on: "It is a difficult decision. Some states have liberalized the abortion laws. If the young person has the funds, she can leave the country to have it performed. The cost can be high. If she elects to have her baby, there are religious charitable institutions that will assist. The emotional consequences can be severe. And with a botched-up abortion, terrible injury or death can be inflicted on the mother. It is a bad situation. Maybe it is due in part to wartime conditions."

My physician friend was wondering out loud. He did not have answers. As a doctor, he must try to be helpful. He did not believe that the older generation could exert absolute control. "The time is past when a teenager—or a girl in her twenties— can be 'commanded'." The only means left are persuasion and education.

Sex Education in School

Sex education is being taught in a number of school districts throughout the country. SIECUS—the Sex Information and Education Council of the United States—is the dominant national organization guiding local school programs. The director of SIECUS is Dr. Mary S. Calderone, a former medical director for Planned Parenthood. SIECUS has come in for criticism. "I'm sure there are some well-intentioned and responsible critics of sex-education programs," Dr. Calderone said. "But we hear almost entirely from the extreme right, which is recruiting the timid and the conservative." [14] When the sex-education program in New York State came under fire, the State Department of Education was quick to point out that it did not mandate a course in sex education. It was up to the individual local school districts to develop such courses, if they wished to do so. Curriculum guidelines and consultants would be provided if requested. However, the State Department of Education does favor and recommend instruction in family life education and human sexuality, but only as a small part of a comprehensive course in the health sciences. "This is an important point which cannot be overstressed—the Department *recommends*—but does not mandate—the teaching of sexuality as a phase in a broad new health program which will go into effect in State classrooms (K-12) during the 1970–71 school year." [15] News releases by the New York State Department of Education have stressed that family health education includes sex education only as a part of a general plan—which includes a massive attack on the problems of alcohol, smoking, and the misuse of drugs.

During 1968–69 a total of 308 pupils in the seventh and eighth grades of Wantagh Junior High participated in a sex-education program. Replies to a student questionnaire to evaluate the course were noteworthy: "Responses to the question of 'What stands out in your mind as the most important thing you learned?' fell into the following major categories: (Number in parentheses denotes number of responses.) How a baby is born (48) How things happen inside the mother (35) Things about the body (35) Information about mating (29) Understanding that growth and sex is natural and wonderful (11) What birth control means (11) Maturity and personality (8) Information about menstruation (4) Information about masturbation (2) Facts about sickness and venereal disease (2) What homosexuality means (1)" [16]

The pupil evaluation further revealed that for a majority of the students the course made them feel more comfortable about their personal growth and sex, as well as providing a great deal of information. Then, too, a majority felt the course helped them to better understand most of their questions about their personal growth and sex.[17] Sex education, properly taught by competent teachers, can aid in personal growth, understanding, and a feeling of comfort in the area of sexuality.

When public school programs are unfairly criticized, the voice of the student can influence local and state educational offices. If you want sex education in your school, you certainly can speak out for it. If the state legislature is hesitant, then letters to assemblymen and congressmen can carry great weight. Lawmakers are responsive to intelligent arguments. The opponents of sex education in the schools have become vocal and often strident. Those who favor such programs should also make their ideas known to those who shape policy. State education departments are concerned about what the public wants. At the present time, most districts teach sex education only to students who have written permission from their parents.

What are the arguments, pro and con?

"I oppose sex education because this is one subject that should be taught at home." Answer: "Sex education in the school does not seek to usurp this function from the parents. Parents can still impart knowledge and attitudes of sex. The school does try to explain the principles of human biology. And, in all honesty, we know that some parents are too shy or embarrassed to answer your questions. In many cases, children, sensing this, do not ask. The question is often not raised."

"I oppose sex education because the teacher may not be qualified. How do I know my child is not learning some sort of perversion?" Answer: "As a parent you have the right to insist that only fully qualified teachers are utilized in the program. Teachers do go through a course of instruction before they actually conduct a class."

"I have heard all sorts of wild stories about what my child is learning in those sex classes." Answer: "Check out the rumors with the teacher. You will find that in most cases the rumors are groundless."

A great deal of mystery still surrounds the process of reproduction. It is one of those flammable issues that can arouse individuals. Occasional mistakes can be made in any educational program. But it is far better for the child to receive sex education in the school than to assimilate misinformation from his friends. Your parents still have the major task to complete in this area of human relations. An enlightened school system can be of valuable assistance.

Your Parents

Most education originates and continues in the home. Within the family you assimilate ideas and attitudes. As you are growing up you expect your parents to be helpful in explaining sexuality. Often the father "explains" matters to the son, and the mother "explains" the facts of life to the daughter. Parents often wait for you to bring up questions about sex. If you do not do so, time passes, and it could happen that you seldom, if ever, get around to discussing this important subject. A story is told of a 10-year-old who asked, "Daddy, where did I come from?" The father then gave a long and involved explanation of how babies are born. "No," said the child, "that's not what I mean. My friend Joe came from Chicago, and Herbert came from New York. I wanted to know where I came from!"

The wise parent anticipates his child's need for sex information and is able to speak to the child at the youngster's level of comprehension. Parents often leave books containing sex information scattered around the house, hoping that you will be curious enough to look at the material and ask for clarification with regard to the subject. If you wish to read up on the subject, you might ask your parents to get you books from the library. Often sex-information books are given by the librarian only to adults.

Be understanding of your parents. Not all adults can discuss the subject with their children. They may lack information, be unsure of how to impart it, or just be too embarrassed or shy to handle the material with you. A teenager once complained, "If my parents can't explain sex to me, they have no right to be parents!" That was a harsh judgment. It would be fine if parents could discuss everything with their children. But their knowledge may be limited. Not every parent can explain the new math to his offspring. Not every parent can give the necessary detailed information about the process of reproduction. That is why sex education in the schools is so necessary and helpful. It does not mean that parents abdicate responsibility by wanting the school to teach about sexuality. The schools can teach the mechanics of human biology. The parents can give guidance in the moral aspects of sex. Sometimes one parent is more adept and at ease in doing so. It is not unusual for one parent to be the source of sex information for all the children in the family.

If a parent cannot fulfill your need for knowledge, you

should be referred to the family physician or a close friend. I know of one situation in which two fathers—both doctors—exchange children to discuss sexuality. Each speaks to the offspring of the other. It works extremely well. That may be an unusual procedure. If a parent simply is unable to talk about sex to his (or her) child, then others in the family—or outsiders—must perform the function.

As a teenager you expect honesty. If a parent is ill-equipped with sexual know-how and information, you should not be too critical. A parent may say in all candor: "Darling, I just cannot explain such matters. But I will arrange for you to see Dr. Smith. He will be happy to answer your questions."

If parents do not bring up the matter of sex, you should do so. If your parents cannot be helpful, ask them to refer you to an adult who can. The alternative is to exchange misinformation with your friends. Unfortunately, few school systems have an organized, ongoing course in sex education and family health. You can urge your school to institute such programs. Adults *do* listen, amazing as it may seem!

It is not only the spoken word that affects your attitude. What you see in the home is a vital consideration. When you see parents who are loving and considerate, you will understand that the sex relationship is a normal part of the human experience. A happy marriage is the best "teacher" you can have. We learn through actions, fully as much as through words. If sex is considered a dirty topic, never to be discussed, then a child will grow up convinced that there is something terrible about it. If sex is a topic of stern moralizing and inspires only fear and contempt, your attitude will be shaped accordingly. If a child senses that performing the sex act is to be done only as a duty to bear children, but not as a source of pleasure, his own feelings about sexuality will be adversely shaped. You hope that your parents will approach the topic of sexuality with candor and openness. Yet you must also be aware that sex is not the easiest subject for parents to discuss.

Variations in Sexual Practices

What is moral in one society is immoral in another. A Moslem is permitted to have four wives. In Western culture, monogamy—one wife for one husband—is the prevalent pattern. The Old Testament declares "Thou shalt not commit adultery." However, the Todas, a non-Hindu tribe in India, say that it is immoral for a husband to withhold his wife from another man.[18] The Todas' practice is not the usual standard for most societies. Polygamy—one husband and two or more wives— was widely practiced in Biblical days among the early Hebrews. Abraham acquired a second wife (called a concubine) when his first wife was unable to bear him a child. Solomon had a palace filled with wives. Historians said that many of his wives were obtained to cement political alliances with neighboring countries. Following the death of Solomon the Jewish kingdom was split when his sons argued over succession rights to his throne.

Societies have permitted multiple wives for a variety of reasons. When the males were killed off in battle, it was necessary to find a place for the surplus women. Extra wives could be helpful in performing domestic duties in the home and in repopulating the tribes decimated by wars. Early civilizations were often structured in such a way that extended kin groups (relatives) were living under one roof. Additional wives could thus be added to the family as the normal pattern of a given culture. The popular picture of a grinning potentate visiting several wives in his harem on a given evening is scarcely the whole story. Polygamy, where tolerated, was usually limited to the rich who could afford extra wives. In most societies that practiced polygamy monogamy was still the more prevalent system in man-woman households. It should also be remembered that a ruler, such as Solomon, had to take ugly as well as attractive brides for his harem. Marriage for political reasons could not be equated with a love relationship.

Sex and Love: Are They the Same?

Americans are excited by the concept of romantic love. Countless films, books, and plays deal with the boy-meets-girl theme. In recent days, films tend to be more explicit. Nude and seminude scenes in films and books offer a frank exposition of the man-woman relationship.

A film such as *I Am Curious (Yellow)* plays to over 250,000 New Yorkers. Despite disapproval by the critics who felt that the movie made sex "boring," many are "curious" to see it. Off Broadway, sexual "overkill" is found in a play titled *Oh! Calcutta!*, in which nakedness is featured—and the box office displays the "sold out" sign every night.

Laws governing pornography have been liberalized. The use of sex in a "significant" social way is legal. Greater freedom of sexual expression prevails. Even the television commercials have strong sexual overtones. Certain deodorants, mouthwashes, or hair sprays are guaranteed to make you more sexually attractive. From the TV sets come the strident voices of hucksters who seek to sell products by making them appear sexy. With a musical theme reminiscent of burlesque house bumps and grinds, a sultry-voiced girl tells you to "take it off." The voice refers to a new brand of shaving cream. A scantily clad Jeannie, who comes out of a bottle, constantly tempts a young military officer with her obvious, yet wholesome, charms. So, in American life, sex can be brazen, or it can tantalize. The communications media—TV, radio, the press, books, magazines—are all hawking the wares of sexiness. It is no wonder that our society is sex-saturated.

While all of this overdone sexuality is thrust upon us, your parents may be seeking to set certain standards of sexual conduct that they consider appropriate.

A teenager declares: "Sex is a private matter. It concerns two individuals. It is none of my parents' business."

Parents are influenced by the Puritan ethic, derived from the Puritans who settled in New England. They possessed a stern code of morality. A woman who committed adultery could be branded with a scarlet letter. Premarital sex resulted in strict penalties. The Pilgrims accepted the literal truth of the Old Testament. A Biblical passage dealing with being stoned to death for harlotry was a guide to punishment. Yet courting couples were allowed to engage in bundling. They could roll about in bed, fully clothed. Often a board would be placed between them. Records show that those colonies permitting bundling did indeed have a higher percentage of illegitimate babies than those that did not.

Despite the sexual freedom found in literature and the arts, Americans tend to be conservative about sexual mores. The politician who is suspected of cheating on his wife may find his career adversely affected. Clandestine romances between political leaders and the "other woman" can still redound to the professional harm of the man in public life. Even during such a dramatic week as the occasion when America landed the first astronauts on the moon, our space pioneers found themselves crowded off the front page by a suspected scandal involving a presidential aspirant who was in an auto mishap with a young campaign worker. Scandal—or suspected scandal— makes the headlines. The senator in question went on national television to declare that he did not have any immoral relations with the young woman. He asked his constituents to help him decide whether to continue his political career. For those who say that America is tolerant of sexual involvement, the shadow cast on Senator Ted Kennedy should cause them to reevaluate their thoughts.

Sex: A Private Matter?

Joseph Fletcher, a Protestant theologian, speaks of "situational ethics." He says that each situation in which you find yourself will create its own definition of what is right or wrong.

The sole criterion should be whether a "loving" situation is involved. Fletcher believes that love is an attitude and not a feeling. Love is what fulfills your humanity. Justice is love distributed. Therefore, love is what is the greatest good for the greatest number of persons. Those who believe in situational ethics would hold that each time you have a relationship with someone, it must be judged on the basis of whether an honest love attitude is engendered. When you are in love, you act as the situation dictates. There are no moral controls. Freedom and fulfillment prevail. Other theologians, such as Paul Ramsey, have argued that love is not enough. You need other principles to establish a relationship.

In actuality, sex is more than a private matter. Parents of the teenager are certainly involved. Teenagers who engage in premarital intercourse may eventually have to confront their parents. If the girl becomes pregnant, then society certainly must be consulted. Shall the couple marry? Are the teenagers mature enough to establish a household? Should the pregnant girl go to a "home" to have her baby? Should she put the child up for adoption, or keep it? Is abortion the answer? Much is said today about having a "meaningful" relationship. Some argue that as long as a boy and girl are having a meaningful relationship, their families should stay out of the picture. That is not always possible.

American religious teachings—be they Protestant, Catholic, or Jewish—are basically geared to sexual intercourse taking place within the framework of marriage. Few would agree with situational ethics. The Old Testament speaks of God commanding Adam and Eve to be "fruitful and multiply." But as time passed and men and women populated the earth, the marriage bed became the proper site of procreation. Judaism and Christianity took a strong stand on fidelity within marriage.

The major Western religions frown on premarital and extramarital sexual intercourse. Even though the new age is freer and more tolerant, sexual deviation from the norms of conduct is not favored. Family and friends still gossip when a bride has a "full-term" baby after being married only five months. Despite the many articles about Scandinavian sexual permissiveness, Americans are not Scandinavians. With all the freedom of sexual expression and lack of censorship, the Puritan code is still evident. No one is branded as an adulteress, but people do talk. Even the most liberal of religious thinkers who speak of situational ethics and meaningful relationships are also quick to point out that the act of love should not deny dignity and humanity to one's partner. Love, they would say, should not be an act of exploitation. To exploit someone else for self-gratification is a violation of even the most liberal moral code. To use another for one's pleasure is clearly exploitative and wrong.

Romantic Love

"And they lived happily ever after." In the movies and plays of the 40's and 50's, the final fadeout showed a boy and girl kissing each other. They had an ecstatic look in their eyes. The only exception was the "horse opera," in which the bashful cowboy tipped his hat to the schoolmarm, mounted his horse, and rode away into the sunset. The schoolmarm smiled bravely with a tear in her eye.

Raoul de Roussy de Sales remarked, "America appears to be the only country in the world where love is a national problem." [19] Definitions of romantic love are difficult to obtain. "Waller and Hill provide us with perhaps as clear a capsule conception of romantic love as we can find: 'Romantic love, as Americans understand it, is an ungovernable impulse, a wholly normal and even sought-for state of grace in which one is unable to think of anything but the loved person—a great tenderness together with the most extreme delusions as to the nature of the loved person—and a striving toward her sometimes attended by extravagances of jealousy and morbid despair if one does not prosper in his suit.' " [20] When romantic love exists, you may feel very possessive toward the object of your affections. You will resent her going out with other boys. If a girl, you may demand that the boy give you his undivided attention. When his eyes wander to a passing miniskirt you may become enraged. You will also idealize your partner. He or she is perfect in your eyes. He or she can do no wrong. She walks with grace. He is handsome and wonderful. You are floating on Cloud Nine. Romantic lovers also want to touch each other constantly. Holding hands in public can be a declaration of possession and warmth of affection. The young girl who sports an engagement ring will proudly show it off to her envious girl friends while with her other hand she has her intended firmly in tow.

Romantic love creates a special problem for the teenager. You are expected to wait until marriage before you have sexual union. Still, what are you to do when the fires of passion are burning? Kissing leads to petting, and petting to more insistent demands—usually from the male—for more complete gratification. The male is taught to be the aggressor in our society. The female does not wish to discourage the male, yet if she gives in she may become known as an "easy mark." She is aware that boys do brag of their sexual conquests. Yet if she is too distant, the boy may not call her again. Many teenage girls try to strike a balance between encouragement and affection, while not going "all the way."

Studies have shown that the ultimate goal of most girls is to attain a happy marriage. Even the girl who is a college graduate will put her job role in a secondary category. Her chief ambition is to become a wife and mother. The female in her teens is developing into a young woman. Girls naturally wish to be attractive to boys. The girl who attracts the most desirable boy on campus is the one who is considered a social success. Girls in college complain that they are confused by their parents' expectations. One girl might say, "When I first went to college, my parents stressed my getting good grades. Now they are concerned because I study too much and do not have enough dates. If I work hard at developing a better social life, my grades will suffer. What shall I do?" Some parents are more

blunt about the matter. They tell their daughters that college
is the best time of their lives to meet and catch a man. They
are encouraged to look harder for Mr. Right than they look
at their textbooks. Society conspires to push the girl toward the
altar. "Mary is already 21 and you mean to tell me she is not
even engaged?" Studies of marriage in America indicate that
boys and girls usually are wed by the time they reach the age
of 22—or 23 at the latest. The push toward the altar begins in
high school. Parents bring subtle pressures to bear. Some encourage their daughters to wear tight, provocative clothes—
even in their early teens—so they can become man-catching
machines. In some communities they hold dancing classes for
9- and 10-year-old boys and girls. The girl who is not popular,
who sits at home waiting for the phone to ring, can become a
social outcast. The overeager mother may lecture the daughter
to be more extroverted—to smile more—to send out signals to
the boys: "You don't have to be in love with a boy to go out
with him. When you are out, you will be seen by other boys.
If you are a clever operator, you can make contacts and get
other dates."

Boys, also, have their problems. Teenage boys tend to wait
until the last minute to ask a girl for a date. When they are
refused, they may think something is wrong with them. Boys
are expected to be aggressive. To be masculine means to be
bold. Society smiles and says, "Boys will be boys." In America,
the double standard prevails. For a teenage boy to have some
sexual experience is not looked upon—by most—as something
unusual. However, a girl who has sexual experience may get
a reputation as a "fast number." As a teenager, you may or
may not mature socially at society's expected rate of development. Just as some teenage girls are slow in developing womanly
figures and interest in boys, so, too, many boys do not mature
socially at the same rate as most of their peers. Not every boy
has taken a girl on a date by the time he has reached his six-
teenth birthday. Sports may be a greater concern than girls.
You may be in the "fantasy" stage in which you talk a lot about

girls while with other boys, yet feel somewhat ill at ease in their presence. The fear of rejection may be very real. A teenage boy can be badly hurt if he calls a girl for a date and receives a blunt refusal. Some boys find it difficult to talk to girls: "I never know what to say. I'm interested in sports. She probably couldn't care less. What do you talk about for a full evening?"

Girls, too, may be shy—where boys are concerned. They may daydream about a handsome boy in the class, yet be petrified and too frightened to speak should the object of their affection suddenly say, "hello." Growing up is not easy. Sexual changes take place within the body as you mature. New desires come to the fore. You think thoughts that you may feel are dirty or nasty. You have fantasies about how nice it would be to have sexual union with a girl (or boy) you see in your class in school. Yet you do not really know even how to begin a relationship. With all the blatant sexuality of our American culture, someone has commented that for Americans, sex is largely a spectator sport. As a teenager you do a lot of looking at the opposite sex. Boys and girls do size each other up.

Ambivalence, too, is a characteristic of romantic teenage love. Today you are madly in love with Jane. A week later you cannot stand her. Mary is now the perfect girl. Like a bee, flitting from flower to flower, many teenagers change partners with great rapidity. Some, however, do go steady rather early in their teens. No two teenagers are ever alike, even as no two children in a given family are ever exactly alike.

Because girls mature physically at a more rapid rate than boys, a girl of 14 may have the figure of a woman, whereas the boy of 14 has yet to have his first shave. It is natural, then, for a 14-year-old girl to seek the attention of a 16-year-old boy. The boys of her own age may be "babies" in her eyes. A 14-year-old girl may tower in height over the boys of her own age. Some girls who are tall for their age slump over to appear smaller, much to the dismay of their mothers.

Romantic love should not be discounted. It is a stage you may go through—and it will carry over into the first few months or years of marriage. "Romantic love may meet still other needs for the adolescent. As a child he found love, warmth, and comfort within his family circle. In fact, within the modern child-centered American family, he was actively conditioned to need love. Yet as he approaches adulthood, life demands that he loosen his ties to his parents; he must emancipate himself. Thus he is confronted with a major predicament. On the one hand, he must relinquish many of his ties with the very people who might meet his love needs. Romantic love provides an answer. It may carry him through a difficult, threatening period until such time as he can establish a home and family of his own. Romantic love functions as a stopgap—as a halfway station." [21]

Another function of romantic love is to help the teenager become emancipated from his home. That does not mean he is rejecting his parents. Rather, he must find ways to loosen the ties to his family so that he will be brave enough to set out on a new course—outside his home—as he prepares for the adult goal of marriage itself. As a teenager matures, he must—of necessity—become more independent. One sign of maturity is to begin to think about the home that you will eventually establish. For a girl to dream of marriage and having children is certainly normal and desirable. The wise parent is aware that someday you will marry and leave home. The teen years are important years in moving in the direction of independence of action—and new adventures. Romantic love is such an adventure!

CHAPTER IV

Changing Sexual Morality

Some persons have said that morality is changing. Surveys would indicate that greater freedom of sexual expression exists today. Studies have shown that premarital virginity is less of a desired goal than it once was held to be. Some studies indicate that girls expect their future husbands to have had some experience before the wedding night. The grooms themselves are less likely to expect their brides to be virgins, especially since many engaged couples have slept together before the wedding ceremony. Studies of college males show that whereas in the 30's and 40's the college male tended to have experience with prostitutes, in the 50's and 60's it seems that he is less likely to do so. He does not need to visit a prostitute, since so many willing partners are available among the female college population. Evidence is also cited to show that on the high-school campus the rate of premarital intercourse is on the rise. Dropping out of high school because of pregnancy is a fairly common event.

Invariably the argument arises: Is there more "sleeping around" than in previous generations—or is it just better publicized? Have young people begun to develop their own moral code of sexual behavior, without the approval of parents or religion or society? Is Puritanism as dead as the dodo? Again, it is difficult to generalize. However, the following factors must be kept in mind.

Religion

Religion has liberalized its approach to the individual. Although some strong (but small) fundamentalist religious sects preach a message of sin, hell, and damnation, such is not the case with most of the Religious Establishment. The Catholic Church is rocked with controversy over the issues of the celibate priesthood, birth control, and abortion. Liberal religious leaders favor liberalizing of the abortion laws. Each religious group has its liberals as well as its conservatives. It would appear that the liberal position is holding sway. Unless a strong reaction sets in, religionists no longer feel they are able to "command" conduct. The best they can do is to educate the young people. Argument and dialogue have replaced authoritarian decisions. The teenager has to be convinced that the old morality is right. The religionist does not point the finger of guilt. He does not say, "You are a fallen woman because you are pregnant and unwed." He does try to be helpful. He may also seek, like the psychiatrist, to relieve you of feelings of guilt. "It is more blessed to forgive than to punish" is the theme of today's American religious norm of conduct. One of the Ten Commandments says, "Thou shalt not commit adultery." The religionist would say that that is a wise law because it makes for the stability of the home. The earlier religionist would have said, "You shall not commit adultery because God commanded it. God knows best. You shall not question His laws."

Psychology and psychiatry have had their effect. The religious leader is more tolerant and understanding. He sees his role as a counselor and comforter. He may be the only one in the community who can refer an unwed pregnant girl to a safe abortionist who will not butcher the youngster.

Religious leaders are uneasy with situational ethics. They find it difficult to make man, and not God, the arbiter of sexual mores. But in the humanistic, secularistic, and pragmatic world of today's America, it is the human element that is uppermost. Religionists are less and less censorious and authoritarian. Man is not yet "the measure of all things." But God is increasingly looked upon as a tolerant Deity, who is more forgiving than wrathful. Roman Catholicism is the only major Western religious faith to hold to a celibate priesthood. Catholics speak of celibacy as a sacrifice incumbent upon the priest. Normal sexuality is not denied to the married couple.

On the college campus, sexual conduct is considered a private affair. It is no longer an issue. Each does his own thing. The college chaplain may be consulted for guidance in sexual matters. However, he is not in a position to render judgment and mete out punishment—even if he wanted to.

Religion still has something to say to America's youth. It says that marriage is the best setting for the fulfillment of sexual desires. The Biblical suggestion that "a man shall leave his parents and cleave to his wife" is still very sensible. Religionists can point out the mental anguish and possible disgrace that face those who violate the sexual codes of society. Life is more than a fulfilling of one's desires. A full life does not demand that we try everything, be it drugs, sex, perversion, murder, or rape.

Religion recognizes the reality of human sexuality. The Interfaith Commission on Marriage and Family Life, sponsored by Catholics, Protestants, and Jews, issued a statement on June 8, 1968. It said in part: "Human sexuality is a gift of God, to be accepted with thanksgiving and used with reverence and joy. It is more than a mechanical instinct. Its many dimensions are intertwined with the total personality and character of the individual. Sex is a dynamic urge or power, arising from one's basic maleness or femaleness, and having complex physical, psychological, and social dimensions. These dimensions, we affirm, must be shaped and guided by spiritual and moral considerations which derive from our Judeo-Christian heritage. The heritage teaches us that the source of values to guide human behavior is in God." [22] Those values are primarily to be taught in the home, and it is a lifelong task, beginning in the earliest years of childhood. The church, synagogue, and school can supplement the values taught in the home. Schools can serve to . . . "integrate sound sexual information and attitudes with the total education which the child receives in social studies, civics, literature, history, home economics, and the biological and behavioral sciences. They can reach the large numbers of young people whose families have no religious identification but who need to understand their own sexuality and their role in society." [23]

Schools should reflect the moral heritage of Western civilization when teaching sexuality. This presents problems, for "where strong differences of opinion exist on what is right and wrong sexual behavior, objective, informed, and dignified discussion of both sides of such questions should be encouraged. However, in such cases, neither the sponsors of an educational program nor the teachers should attempt to give definite answers or to represent their personal moral and religious beliefs as the consensus of the major religions or of society generally." [24] The foregoing ecumenical statement highlights the difficulty faced by religion in sex education.

The three faiths agree that God is the source of moral values, and the home is the primary place to be taught sexuality. Sex education in the schools is to reflect moral values while not offending anyone's religious sensibilities. Since religions do differ on attitudes toward birth control and abortion, the schoolteacher is placed in a difficult position when seeking to answer questions. The interfaith statement is an example of the difficulty faced by religion when confronted with the moral and ethical values associated with sex. Parents are uneasy about the potential danger of the sex-education teacher acting in the role of clergyman, when imparting information in such a delicate area. The interfaith statement points out that sex education ". . . should teach that sexuality is a part of the whole person and an aspect of his dignity as a human being. It should teach that people who love each other try not to do anything that will harm each other. It should teach that sexual intercourse within marriage offers the greatest possibility for personal fulfillment and social growth." [25]

Sociology

The sociologist studies the patterns of human behavior. He does not render a judgment. He describes how people act. Religionists and philosophers can then take the raw data he compiles and reach value judgments. Sociologists take samplings, ask questions, run tests, and try to "tell it like it is." Alfred Kinsey found ". . . that 91 per cent of the women and 89 per cent of the men in his sample had engaged in premarital petting by the age of 25. [Winston] Ehrmann, in a study of the premarital sexual behavior of 1,423 college students, found that 97 per cent of both men and women engage in some form of premarital petting. But for 13 per cent of the men and 44 per cent of the women, the most intensive form of petting that they had engaged in was kissing and hugging. Some 57 per cent of the men, aged 18 through 21, and 13 per cent of the women, aged 18 through 22, reported premarital intercourse." [26]

Ernest W. Burgess and Paul Wallin did a sociological study of native-born, college-level, urban Protestants and found that although fewer men than women were virgins at marriage, the trend toward a decrease in virginity had been halted. Many of the nonvirgins had premarital relations with their future husbands. Only a small increase took place in the figures pertaining to women who had premarital intercourse with men other than their future husbands. The same held true for men. Burgess and Wallin indicated in their studies that although premarital intercourse has increased in the past few decades, much of it occurs between partners who eventually wed.[27]

Sociologists have found that ". . . there appear to be four formal standards of premarital sex behavior in America; abstinence, the double standard, permissiveness with affection, and permissiveness without affection. Of the four, the double standard, which is fraught with inconsistencies, may be the most widespread." [28] The double standard means that boys are permitted to have sexual intercourse before marriage, but girls are not to do so. Thus, one standard of conduct holds for males and a stricter one for females.

Sociologists continue to study the sexual behavior of males and females in American society. In general, they have noted an increase in sexual intercourse at the high-school and college level. However, the sexual behavior varies according to one's educational attainment. Kinsey's studies revealed that college-trained men and women had less sexual experience than their working counterparts.

A sociologist cannot tell you how to act. He can only give you the results of his studies, showing what is actually occurring in society. The fact that he has discovered that people act in a given way does not make that particular conduct either right or wrong.

Psychology

The psychologist is concerned with what goes on in your mind. Sigmund Freud felt that many of our problems stem from earliest childhood. He was concerned with man's fears and frustrations and guilt feelings. Much of these he traced to sexual problems and fantasies. A psychologist does not pass moral judgment. He cannot say that one action is right and another wrong. He studies what gives you peace of mind, and what is upsetting to you. He is concerned with how well you adjust to society—and how well you can live with the tensions, anguish, and frustrations of day-to-day life.

The psychologist and psychiatrist try to help the patient to solve his own problems. For example, if an unwed pregnant teenager comes to see the psychiatrist, he will try to get her to decide what she really wants to do. Shall she have her baby or shall she have an abortion? Shall she put the child up for adoption or keep it? Shall she seek to force the father to marry her? How can she cope with her parents, who are heartbroken and angry? The psychiatrist will try to help the young person to live with the reality of the situation—and to arrive somehow at a satisfactory solution to the many difficulties and problems inherent in her situation. Hopefully, the girl is given some insight as to why she behaved as she did. Psychiatry is not a cure-all. It can be helpful to those who willingly seek guidance.

Psychiatrists tend to be basically nondirective (they do not give many answers—they tend to point you in certain directions). Psychiatrists seek to bring you to the point of having the ability to make mature judgments, free of excessive guilt. Even here—on the subject of guilt—psychiatrists disagree. Some feel that legitimate guilt can be healthy, and will thus prevent you from repeating your mistakes. Others seek to remove all feelings of guilt.

Psychiatrists and religionists differ in discussing the matter of conscience. Is there "a still small voice that says 'thou shalt' or 'thou shalt not'?" Does conscience arise from human experiences (learning right from wrong by trial and error) or does it stem from the Divine? Do we behave because we fear our parents, friends, or the law? Does ethical behavior spring from the Commandments of God? Do our actions spring from ideas and emotions buried deep within the human mind? Those are some of the unresolved questions that you will grapple with as you grow toward maturity.

Teen Surveys

Several years ago I attended a Religious Youth Conclave weekend during which we conducted a survey of teenage attitudes toward a variety of subjects, one of which was sexual conduct. Seventy-three campers were involved, their average age 16. Thirty-three were males and forty were females. The results were of interest. Forty-two percent said they had petted heavily, 40 percent said they had close friends of the opposite sex who were not virgins, 83 percent beileved that a girl should be a virgin before marriage, but only 38 percent expected a boy to be. Some 35 percent felt it would be right for an engaged couple to have intercourse, and 33 percent said they personally would see nothing wrong in their having intercourse with their fiancées. However, only 18 percent believed that it would be right for a couple to have intercourse if they were just dating. When the figures were broken down in the male and female category, it turned out that 67 percent of the boys felt a girl should be a virgin before marriage, whereas 85 percent of the girls held that view. This limited survey would indicate that girls treasure virginity higher than do boys. Fifteen percent of the girls admitted to not being virgins, and 33 percent of the boys claimed the same status. Of the boys, 60 percent said they had petted heavily, whereas 35 percent of the girls said they did so. The survey sampling would seem to bear out the contention that teenage boys are more sexually experienced than are girls—at least as far as this survey of white, middle-class, suburban teenagers was concerned. Since it was an anonymous, voluntary survey that was intended to inform the conclavers of the mores of its own participants, we may assume that it was honestly compiled.

After the results of the survey were tabulated, the youth leaders and rabbis led a discussion on changing sexual morality patterns. Frankness and openness characterized the discussion. Probing questions were raised as to the religious attitude toward virginity, the double standard, and even as to the sex act itself. It was clearly evident to the adult leadership that this was a topic of great interest—and at the same time much ignorance was found as to the basic facts of sexuality. The discussion went into depth as to Judaism's stand on premarital sexual intercourse. The replies of the survey indicated that whereas 83 percent of the campers favored premarital chastity for a girl at marriage, only 38 percent expected such chastity of a boy. The double standard (permissive for a boy, restrictive for a girl) was borne out in the camper survey.

More extensive surveys of sexual practices have revealed that sexual intercourse is widely practiced by high-school students. The Connecticut State Department of Health issued the results of a survey taken in 1966. The survey showed that one 13-year-old girl in every six in Connecticut will become pregnant out of wedlock before she reaches her twentieth birthday. Since every sixth girl becomes pregnant, many more must be assumed to have intercourse without becoming pregnant.

Recognizing the dimensions of the problem, adult and teenage forum discussions were held in the Hartford area. Dr. Mary S. Calderone of the Sex Information and Education Council of the

United States (SIECUS) spoke to one of the forums. She pointed out that there is much more to sexuality than having sexual intercourse. She held that there could be warm and friendly relationships between boys and girls who do not indulge in sexual intercourse. Dr. Calderone said, "Sexual experience isn't a right, to be claimed as soon as puberty sets in. It's a privilege, to be earned only by the achievement of a certain amount of emotional maturity and a minimum amount of chronological maturity. We set ages for legal majority, for voting, for driving licenses. Why are we afraid to say forthrightly, 'While you're still in high school, you're just plain too young in every way to make the mature judgments and decisions that this important step requires'?" [29]

At the Connecticut Sexuality Forums, teenagers raised the following questions:

> "There are a few girls around the neighborhood who will let you do anything to them. Is it completely wrong to play along with them?"
>
> "What is the limit that a boy and girl can do together?"
>
> "Is feeling a girl as bad as sexual intercourse?"
>
> "When a man and woman want to have intercourse, do they wear anything on the parts that connect?"
>
> "How can a girl, after being a virgin all her life, change her morals when she gets married?" [30]

The above are some of the real questions that trouble many teenagers today. The lack of standards and the absence of authority have led many to develop sexual morality on a "situational" basis. Many seem to follow Joseph Fletcher, who says that love or affection is the ultimate standard, and that we do not bring any preconceived notion to any relationship (including the sexual). Each contact is to be judged on whether it is loving or beneficial. With the absence of authority, anything goes!

The Connecticut Sexuality Forums indicate that a great deal of ignorance exists about the facts of sex. Teenagers and parents are confused. Sex education for both the parents and their children would be very helpful.

Threats Do Not Work

At one time, virtuous behavior could be ensured by the fear of conception, infection, or detection. The pregnant teenager has discovered—often to her sorrow—that she did conceive. Even with all proper precautions, no contraceptive device is 100 percent foolproof. Rates of infection from venereal disease are once again on the rise, despite the availability of penicillin and other drugs. Detection still occurs, despite the use of automobiles and motels. So, although some teenagers feel "safe" in having sexual intercourse, possible consequences are still to be faced. Abortion laws are not changing rapidly. Only a handful of states have liberalized their abortion procedures.

Fear of pregnancy is real. Often the mother is as fearful as her daughter. A mother asks, "My teenage daughter is going off to college in the fall. She has asked me for permission to take the Pill. What should I do?"

A teenager thinks to herself, "I would like to be able to get the pills if I need them. Shall I ask my mother what I should do? Will she be angry with me?"

To use or not to use the Pill—that is often a vital question. The use of the Pill can prevent unwanted pregnancy. In the free atmosphere on many college campuses, girls feel they must have contraceptive devices. Many men's dorms have virtually eliminated the curfew. It is not unusual for a girl to stay overnight in a man's room. Most colleges no longer exert much control *in loco parentis*. They simply do not act in the parent's place. Deans say that the purpose of the college is to educate, not to set moral standards of sexual conduct. More and more, college officials are coming to the conclusion that sexual morality is a private affair, and does not concern the university. A girl from Barnard and a boy from Columbia made news in the papers when they publicly proclaimed they were living together, in defiance of the university ban on unmarried couples' sharing an apartment. They flouted the law openly, because they felt there was too much hypocrisy. The law was on the books. It was not enforced. A number of unwed college student couples were living together. This particular couple decided to make a test case of the matter. After an uproar lasting several weeks, the only penalties initially imposed were that the couple involved were not allowed to eat at the school cafeteria and could not attend the school's social dances. When a newspaper reporter interviewed the father of the boy in the case, the father was more concerned about his son's losing his draft deferment, because of falling grades, than he was about his boy's female roommate.

What shocked school officials only five or six years ago would hardly cause a ripple of excitement today. Co-ed dorms are to be found in many parts of the country. Students have convinced the school authorities that if they are old enough to be drafted, they are old enough to set their own standards of sexual conduct. This new spirit of assertiveness is prevalent on many campuses. "Make love, not war" is the cry of the campus protester. His less vocal brother and sister on campus may well be following the same advice. Some students claim that there is less immoral conduct where co-ed dorms are in use. The absence of rules and the granting of greater freedom has led to more responsibility. One student told me that on his campus sexual promiscuity decreased when co-ed dorms and open hours for visitation became the accepted practice. "If we are treated like adults, we will act like adults." Mixed dorms do not breed romance. Proximity and constant contact in co-ed dorms have downgraded glamour and mystery. That is what many college students will tell you.

Chaplain Richard Israel of Yale speaks of the old "new" morality. According to Chaplain Israel, this means the college student says, "I must trust my own instincts. I want instant gratification. I can do what I wish." He holds that the term "new morality" is simply not used anymore on the campus. It is a microethical issue (a matter of small concern). Israel says the issue is pretty much settled! Sexual conduct is a private matter.

It is not discussed very much. College officials are not terribly concerned. It would appear that the issue has been settled—at least for the moment—in terms of permissiveness.

A college student is mature enough to conduct his (or her) sex life as he (or she) sees fit. Israel said that last year's parent would say, "Our daughter? We gave her the Pill." This year the same parent would declare, "Yes, we gave her bail money." Sex is now a small issue, largely settled. The old "new" morality said "make love, not war." The new "new" morality is concerned with politics, and the ethics of the big issues. Dow Chemical recruiters are a bigger issue than curfew in the men's dorm. Israel sees sex as a microethical issue, whereas pacifism, war, and the draft are macroethical concerns. The latter are major, the former minor. He compares the attitude of modernist religionist thinking on sex to the story of the three bears' porridge—not too hot (overly concerned) not too cold (completely unconcerned), but just right. College students have three attitudes toward the new sexual morality: It is against the law of nature; it is against the law of the land; or "I can't get any of it." Chaplain Israel feels that sexual patterns have changed, but not as much as the talk about them. Certainly there is more rhetoric and discussion of the new morality.

The Dating Game

It is no mistake when Americans speak of "The Dating Game." On television the game is played as a young man asks questions of three lovely girls whom he cannot see. After some bantering back and forth, the male decides which of the girls he would like to have as his date. The dating game program violates one of the cardinal principles of boy-meets-girl. The boy is not permitted to select his date on the basis of appearance. He has selected her only on the basis of her personality, as reflected in her voice and her giggle. Computer dating offers the same difficulty. Information is fed into a machine. Compatibility is measured in terms of common interests, backgrounds, likes, and dislikes. However, it is only when the couple actually meet that the chemistry of attraction or disinterest will come into focus. The dating game and computer dating have aspects of the blind date about them. The ultimate test is to be found in how well the couple get along once they are together.

Sociologists have discovered many different kinds of dating: group dating, double dating, casual dating, serious dating, social dating, and going-steady dating. To go steady for a 13-year-old is not the same as for an 18-year-old. Margaret Meade, the sociologist, has said that dates are mutually exploitative. Each seeks to gain something from the arrangement. The girl may use the boy to meet other young men. The male may use the girl in the sense that he dates her to show her off to his friends, and thus to impress them with his ability to date the cutest and most popular girl in town.

Studies have shown that most married couples select their partners within a radius of some 20 to 50 miles of their own residence. Proximity is still a major factor in the dating game. For the teenager who lacks a car, it becomes a necessity. A boy finds more satisfaction in dating a girl he can walk to the movies than in dating a girl who lives farther away. Who wants one's father to drive him around? In urban areas, where public transportation is more easily available, distance may not be as drastic a factor.

The automobile makes a big difference in dating. In the film *Goodbye, Columbus,* the young man is able to court a girl from a higher income bracket because he has a car. He has the mobility to drive out to the Country Club as the guest of his girl friend. The novella, *Goodbye, Columbus,* was written in the 1950's. It created quite a stir at the time. People were shocked to read of a middle-class, college-age couple who were having extensive coitus although unmarried. The girl used a diaphragm and was upset when her mother discovered it while cleaning out her bureau. Philip Roth leaves it to the reader's imagination as to whether the girl left it in the drawer so it could be discovered— and thus give her an excuse not to renew her passionate summer romance—or if the diaphragm was left at home by mistake. The young man questions the girl closely as to why she did not take it with her when she went back to college (since theirs was a summer romance). She offers some vague excuse that if she needed it, she would go home some weekend to get it. When Roth wrote his book, the Pill was not in general use, and there was some question as to how extensively college girls used diaphragms. In the 50's girls were less likely to discuss such topics with their parents. The film, made in the 60's, is somewhat dated, since it dwells on the sense of shock and horror that the girl's parents exhibit when they discover their daughter's heated summer liaison. The story indicates that the girl breaks off the romance by leaving the diaphragm where the mother will find it. She tells the boy that she simply cannot have him home for Thanksgiving dinner. "How would it look to bring you in the house, when my parents know what we were doing all summer?" A deeper reason—as presented in the film—seems to be that the girl wished to break off the relationship because the young man lacked ambition and had no set goals. As a somewhat spoiled young woman, she was seeking a good provider—as well as an expert lover.

The Graduate was another film—made somewhat earlier—that dealt with the theme of the young college graduate who is confused about contemporary sexual mores. His clumsy attempt to make a hotel reservation for an older woman and himself was a masterpiece of pathos tinged with humor. The moral issue is raised when the young man falls in love with the daughter of the woman he has been sleeping with. He cannot understand the mother's being upset. He wonders why he is unfit to pursue the daughter, simply because he has had an affair with the mother. The affair was largely instigated by the bored mother, who was looking for some action. The fact that the young girl is engaged to the fraternity stud, who is a big ladies' man, does not disturb the girl's mother. The young graduate has entered into a world of great confusion. He cannot understand the moral postures of his parents' generation. If there is a moral to *The Graduate* it would seem to be that keeping up appearances is the true meas-ure of moral worth. The moral would be that a young man who sleeps with his future mother-in-law is looking for trouble. Even his weak protestation that when he had the affair with the mother he had not yet met the daughter was to no avail. He had broken with an accepted cultural pattern.

Even though the American family is "nuclear," films such as *The Graduate* and *Goodbye, Columbus* indicate that dating can-not be divorced from parental approval or disapproval. When it comes to marriage, the sociologists have shown statistically that the chances for success are greatest when a couple is from the same religious, cultural, social, and ethnic background. A very wise rabbi once told me that in marriage the couple should be the same in every way—except that one is a boy and the other a girl. When the passion of romantic love cools a bit, the couple suddenly discover that they have to live with each other as they share the common concerns, hopes, and dreams of life. If their life-styles and expectations are radically different, the marriage may fall apart.

Studies reveal that a wife should not excel her husband in financial achievement. The man who sees his wife forge ahead while his career languishes may be unable to tolerate the mar-riage. His ego may suffer too much. The Hollywood female star who outshines her husband is a familiar figure. When the glam-our of the dating game wears off, and the marriage vows have been exchanged, then the problems of adjustment begin. Men who have married for money may discover that when they cease to amuse, their wives may regard them with contempt.

The dating game is just that. It is a stylized American form of boy-meets-girl. It often leads to engagement and marriage. The problem in contemporary American life has to do with whether the rules have changed. For some, the rules are now changed in-deed. Necking and petting are not enough. The males demand more—and surprisingly enough, some studies have shown that it is often the female who is the aggressor in seeking to go all the way. In certain circles a devil-may-care attitude prevails toward the risk of pregnancy. In *Goodbye, Columbus* the young man is shocked to learn that his girl friend has not been taking precautions. He screams at her in disgust and asks what makes her think that because she comes from a fine home in a lovely neighborhood she cannot become pregnant. The girl appears unconcerned. Only under protest does she get "fitted." She admits to having taken the Pill for a time, but found it made her feel sick. A more contemporary term is "lucking out," meaning to take one's chances on a possible pregnancy.

Society seems to expect the girl to be more giving. A penalty arises only if the Pill does not work. Moral judgments are pronounced if she becomes pregnant. Novelists and playwrights have fostered the idea that intercourse is just one more healthy bodily function—like eating or sleeping or playing basketball. Nudity becomes a healthy way to parade around the stage or across the screen in the movie house. Laws of pornography are freely and loosely interpreted. Censorship is practically gone. Films are rated—and movie-goers flock to those having an "x" rating. The uni-sex mode of dress seeks to obliterate the distinction between boy and girl. The couple who stroll down the street look alike. The only difference: the boy's hair is longer! In an earlier age, society frowned on the "fast" girl. Today, the girl who dispenses her favors to every male in sight is still looked down upon. However, the girl who is intimate on a regular basis with her steady boy friend is not condemned. Even if the liaison does not lead to marriage, the girl's conduct is subject to little disapproval.

Why do young unmarried couples sometimes have intercourse? Often, the boy has many years of college ahead of him. He is not financially able to support a wife. His parents are struggling to raise the funds to send him to college. The college diploma has become a requirement for advancement in this technological age. It is the passport that will open the doors of employment. A teenager who is a freshman in college does not wish to wait. He raises the moral question, "Is it better for me to go to a prostitute for relief, or for me to have relations with a nice college girl?" The traditional moral answer would be to consider the virtue in waiting. He will reply, "Is it better to masturbate than to have sexual intercourse?"

In an earlier age, continence until marriage was the norm for many of the males and for a majority of the females. Today relationships in the dating game tend to ripen rather quickly. Intimacy is a private matter. It is not the concern of society. It would seem that society gets involved only when a girl becomes pregnant. Even then, the girl is given pity and compassion and counsel. She is not branded as immoral. A generation ago, when a movie star was involved in a sex scandal, his career could be ruined. Today, young actresses and actors live together—and jet from one country to another, making films and giving interviews—and there is no sense of shame. The youth who reads of such exploits and finds they are not condemned begins to wonder—shall I not see, and do likewise? Not many have the courage or will power to swim against the tide. The sexual currents are swift in our day. They rush out to a "sea of permissiveness."

It is no wonder teenagers are often confused. American society still expects chastity. The Puritan tradition still runs deep. But the public exhibition of sex is otherwise. Someone has called the decade just passed the "sexy sixties." The home and religion still remain as the strongest forces for an earlier code of morality. The government has given way on many matters involving sexuality. The colleges refuse to legislate sexual conduct. No one can predict what the future will bring.

What Shall You Do?

I would make the following suggestion to today's teenager:

First, do not be misled. It is not always true that what you hear is actually taking place. As far as boys are concerned, we know that young men tend to brag about sexual exploits that often have never taken place. Remember that sensationalism is good box office. Theater tickets do not always deliver what is promised in the coming attractions. Sexuality sells toothpaste, books, films, and cars. Sexuality has become an exploitable product. Often it is oversold. Remember that boys are expected to be aggressive. That is part of masculinity. A girl must be careful to distinguish between a good "line" and sincerity. She must be wary of the smooth salesman who covets her favors. It is still true today that men gossip and brag about conquests. Be critical of the "playboy" philosophy that looks upon girls as love objects to be used and then discarded.

Second, it is not necessary to follow the crowd if you have a different standard. If you look around, you will find others who share your ideas, ideals, and concerns. Speak to your parents. Consult with your minister. Talk to others with an opposite view. To do your own thing in the area of sex does not mean that you must do as you think others are doing.

Third, retain an open mind. Be critical. Ask. Look. Examine your own thoughts and feelings. Teenage is a time of turbulence. The boy you love today may be the boy you cannot bear to be with tomorrow. In growing up, your physical growth may surpass your mental and emotional development. Give your mind a chance to catch up with your body.

Fourth, do not panic. The fact that most of your friends are engaged does not mean that you must cast your moral standards to the winds in the frantic rush to get a boy or girl to the altar. Pressures are exerted by well-meaning parents and friends. But remember that the choice is yours to make. Do not place that choice in the hands of others. A sign of maturity is the willingness to make a decision—and to stick by it.

Fifth, before reaching a decision on sexual conduct, examine the possible consequences of your actions. For the girl, being an unwed mother is a source of tears and regret. For the boy, the prospect of a "shotgun wedding" and ruined career are living options. It is not only the girl who may have to pay the penalty. The boy who marries the girl out of a sense of duty may find that his life is destroyed. He may have to leave school to support his wife and child. Crushed dreams do not offer a happy prospect for marital bliss.

Sixth, do not be afraid to wait. Studies reveal that the most successful marriages occur when the couples are wed in their middle or late 20's. The teenage marriage is fraught with peril. Statistically, teenagers have small chance for success in wedlock. Years later, couples are likely to regret not having finished college and getting started in the world of work before getting married.

Seventh, be aware that the ultimate decision is yours to make. Weigh the factors carefully. Maturity demands a consideration of what your values might be. To live means to have goals. What are the things you cherish? How are life's purposes related to your moral standards? How much are you willing to compromise with what you believe in your heart?

Those are but a few of the questions that come to mind, as one approaches the new morality. Further, one wonders if the new morality is really new. After all, many centuries ago it was the Spartans who worshipped the body. The Greeks had reverence for the naked form. Those civilizations eventually crumbled, when each person decided to do his own thing. The fall of Rome occurred when the people became fat, lazy, and indolent. When hedonism—living for personal pleasure—took over, the state began to crumble. The sociologist Carle C. Zimmerman calls this the final stage of a civilization. He uses the term the "atomistic" family. In such a family, each individual lives for his own happiness. Like the Epicureans, each says, "eat, drink, and be merry, for tomorrow we may die." Zimmerman holds that when the family moral structure collapses, the state itself is in a stage of decay.

Your private acts do have social repercussions. You are part of a family and a community. Sexual activity is not a completely private concern. You cannot entirely divorce yourself from your environment. Life involves people. You are not alone. We do interact with others. Meaningful relationships involve more than the two partners to a love affair.

Be aware that as a teenager you are beginning to prepare for marriage. Your romantic thoughts project you into a future, to be shared with one whom you will love.

Love and Sex

There is a difference between love with affection and love without affection. Robin Stone, in *The Love Machine,* is a man who cannot truly love anyone until he comes to terms with himself. The Robin Stones of Jacqueline Susann's novel are unfulfilled and incomplete. To love is to need another person. Love is much more than the act of sexual intercourse. The pages of *The Love Machine* are filled with incidents of coitus. Yet it is, for the most part, merely a series of orgasms. Love without affection goes nowhere. It ultimately degrades those who practice it. Love with affection leads to a needing and a giving relationship.

Western religions have fostered a moral code that speaks of love and sex within the bonds of matrimony. Marriage is considered a Divine commandment. The authority cited is God, rather than man. Sigmund Freud spoke of freedom and the need to be rid of repression and guilt. Charles Darwin declared that man shared a common ancestor with the ape. Karl Marx spoke of a socialist society in which religion would no longer dictate the norms of conduct. Freud, Darwin, and Marx helped to pave the way for what is now called the new morality. The liberated man was a product of accident or chance, whose origins were shrouded in mystery. In his striving for survival, he would become "whole" as he threw off the restraints of "repressive" religion. Freud substituted the authority of the mind for God. Darwin replaced the Divine with scientific theories as to the origin of the species. Marx fashioned the State as the Lord of the technological age. Social philosophers analyze the future of morality in terms of procreation without intercourse, in a world of test-tube babies. The outlines of such a future can be only dimly seen.

Whatever the future may hold in store for man, we are aware

that the teenager lives very much in the here and now. Your problems are real. Temptations and opportunities do exist. To speak of sexual conquests and sexual prowess is to boast of sex—without love. The new morality seeks to separate sex from love. Sex is animal passion, to be enjoyed by men and women alike. It is a sport that all can play. It has little to do with love—with lasting affection. Love demands giving. Pure sex can become self-serving, offering only momentary pleasure. Is living for the moment sufficient? You will have to make that decision.

A full life demands a set of values. What are your values? Are they self-centered? How concerned are you about your fellow man? Does the crowd set your standards? How much of an *individual* are you willing to be?

CHAPTER V

The New Morality and the Mass Media

"Education is how kids learn stuff." That is how one youngster defined the process of acquiring knowledge. You learn a lot of "stuff" on TV. A college professor, Marshall Mc-Luhan, has said that "the medium is the message." He indicated that the medium itself, be it TV, radio, films, or the press, seems to have a reality of its own. It is as if TV were more than a creation of science. By its being there, it not only transmits, it also influences what we see and hear. As Shakespeare said, "The play [medium] is the thing [to] catch the conscience of the king."

John M. Culkin, S.J., declared, "Not all of McLu is nu, or tru." [31] It is difficult to accept the idea that TV should have a personality of its own. Yet we know that TV does make news. A demonstrator who stands before a TV camera is transformed from obscurity to instant leadership. McLuhan now says, "The medium is the *massage*." It does affect our thinking and our actions. To some extent, the content of what we see on TV is influenced by the form of communication. The medium is not neutral. It is alive.

How should we understand the new ways of communicating? Edward T. Hall believes that art and technology are extensions of man. Man invented the stone ax as an extension of his hand. The wheel was discovered to supplement the foot. Glasses were to help our eyes to see. So, inanimate objects—an ax, wheel, or glasses, do have a distinctive function as an extension of man himself. McLuhan would say that this tends to give them a reality of their own. Television does not just project images. The TV camera is, in a sense, alive. It is an extension of the man behind

78

it. In a TV studio, they say, "Look into the live camera." The camera that is on has the property of life itself.

In time, life begins to imitate art. That means we tend to copy what we see on television or in films. Johnny Carson wears a certain style of suit. Soon, a million viewers are purchasing similarly tailored garments. A film star dresses in a certain way. Many will copy her mode of dress. A rock group appears on television. Others form groups to imitate their dress or sound. The medium—be it TV, film, or records, aids in setting the pace. If we think in terms of morality, the medium is indeed the "massage." It massages us. It stirs us up. Excessive nudity in films can influence our moral attitudes toward sex. Pornography in books is also a medium. It conveys a message. It says that such sexuality exists. If it exists, it may not be immortal.

McLuhan distinguishes between a "hot" and a "cool" medium. Photography, film, radio, TV, are "hot." A seminar is "cool." The hot medium is one in which you do not talk back. The cool medium invites participation. According to McLuhan's definition, it would appear that the hot media have tremendous effect upon us.

A danger lies in Dr. McLuhan's ideas. They may give to an inanimate object more importance than it really has. Men do invent machines. The TV cameras are operated by human beings. The ideas that are presented arise from situations involving men in their struggle to live—and to find a meaning in their existence.

Not all would agree with McLuhan. The late Martin Buber, Jewish teacher and author, taught that all life was "meeting." However, he said, there were two types of meeting. One he called "I—It." This occurred when a person met another person in a casual manner without really caring too much about the other individual. Buber cited as an example the doctor who looks upon his patients as a series of "cases" rather than whole individuals who need to be treated on a very personal, intensive, individual basis. Most of our lives are spent with the I—It relationship. However, when we relate in an intensive way to someone else (and not to a thing, such as a TV set) we experience "I—Thou." At that moment, said Buber, God is present at our meeting. I—Thou is rare for most people. When you think about it, how many I—Thou friends will you have in a lifetime? Someone has said that the number of true friends you acquire in a lifetime can be counted on the fingers of one hand. For McLuhan, a discussion would be considered "cool," since there is a give and take. If such a discussion contains the magic of sincere communication with another person, then Buber would say it is "I—Thou."

Martin Buber has appealed to religious thinkers of all faiths. His idea that life is dialogue and confrontation has wide appeal. Buber would not have been likely to credit the radio with anything more than I—It. For him, the radio or TV would be impersonal. He felt you could only relate dynamically to another individual. He did say that sometimes a person could I—Thou with an animal. He recalled an incident of his youth on a farm. He gave a horse a cube of sugar. As the horse snuggled near him, there was a magic moment of communion. He called it an I—Thou experience. It was intense and unusual, although it lasted only a fleeting moment.

The medium codifies reality. It tells us what happens. Let us apply McLuhan's thinking to an actual situation. The TV cameras follow Lee Harvey Oswald as he is taken to his jail cell. Suddenly a shot rings out. Oswald is killed. There is panic and confusion. We have seen the event on our TV screens. It happened in an instant. Later the press wrote extensively about the event. It may take thousands of words to describe what occurred. The visual is as real (if not more so) than the written word.

When commentary is added to pictures, a formidable force is created. For if the newscasters on the medium analyze in too much detail, they may be criticized for biased reporting. Government officials are sensitive to the influence of television commentators. They feel that they *make* the news at times, instead of reporting it. For some, TV is not a hot medium (when no dialogue takes place). Rather it is a cool medium that is alive and stimulates and influences—perhaps unduly. McLuhan is not easy to understand. In the age of multimedia, he is trying to describe what happens to us when our senses are bombarded by a number of forces.

While attending a religious convention, I dropped in on a "multimedia" religious service. Five screens were mounted on a stage. Five cameras were simultaneously projecting pictures. The theme of the service was love. The five screens were continuously busy. On one was a peaceful sunset. On another some animals were at play. On a third two young people walked hand in hand. The other two screens showed nature scenes. While the five films were being shown, a guitarist played and sang a song of love and friendship. When his melody ended, a rabbi read a poem about love between a boy and girl as a reflection of the love that man has for God. During the presentation, the congregation joined in singing a familiar hymn. It was a multimedia service because it sought to reach the congregation on a variety of levels at the same time. Most of the senses were engaged. It had a tremendous impact on the worshippers.

It may well be that the religion of the future will use pictures instead of sermons. The techniques of multiscreens, as used at the New York World's Fair and Canada's Expo 67, may be the wave of the future.

There is no doubt that the medium has the power to "massage" our senses. We live in a world of images. A teacher told me the following: "I find I have to use a great deal of film and records in my classes. The youngsters are attuned to visual impressions. Books are of lesser interest. It may be that McLuhan is right. My generation read books. The new generation sees films and listens to recordings."

The End of Thrift?

It appears that the mass media are creating a new morality. The media stimulate the taste of the buying public. The media "massage" us to buy things we do not need. Buber said, "All

life is meeting." Modern man seems to be meeting the media—
and finding there a commercial message.

The teenage market generates the sale of millions of dollars
worth of merchandise. Credit cards for teenagers are becoming
more and more common. The American economy is largely
built on credit. "Buy now, pay later." It was not always so.

In Colonial times, the Puritan New England tradition in
America preached thrift and saving one's money. "A penny
saved is a penny earned." Impulse buying was considered evil.
Rapid change in styles of dress, or modes of thought, were condemned. Hard work, saving for a rainy day, loyalty to one's job
and class in society—those were the early American virtues.
New-fangled ideas were frowned upon. Youth was a time to
prepare for the responsibilities of the adult world. Money was
not freely given to the teenager. Parents had little to give. Excessive advertising would be considered the work of the devil. Now
we hear ads on the radio telling us in a New England twang to
purchase rolls like "Grandma used to make." Just warm them up.
No need exists to make your own bread.

Before the Industrial Revolution, the home was the "factory."
Mother cooked, baked, and made her own clothes. The father
worked the small farm near the house in which the family lived.
The children did chores in and about the home. Much of the
food was grown on the family farm. Education was nearby, at
the one-room schoolhouse. Frugality was the order of the day.
There was no "extra" money. There were no price supports
for farmers. A bad crop—the result of adverse weather conditions—could spell disaster. The Industrial Revolution changed
all that. The young people went out, became educated, and took
jobs far from home. Factories generated jobs, money, and, with
the rise of unions, more leisure time because of a shorter work
week. On the early farms, fun was had at home as the family
gathered around the player piano. Today the teenager will go
out for a ride in the family car to a discothèque or a drive-in
movie, or meet his friends at the candy store. It is a different
world. Your room at home may be filled with gadgets. The mark

of success is not in how fast you harvest the crop, but rather how high are your grades at school. If you do live on a farm, chances are it is highly mechanized.

Machines have replaced men. Colleges train you for highly technical skills. New careers open up daily. Forty years ago, who would have applied for a position as a computer operator? In the next decade we may have jobs in space medicine, with patients being treated at outer space stations to measure their reaction to weightlessness. A whole new industry is growing up around space technology. New jobs are generated by every advance that is made in the field of science.

Thoughtful educators and clergymen are now taking a second look at the morality of promotion. How far is it legitimate for advertisers to go in influencing the public mind? The most dramatic case concerns the tobacco industry. Gradually cigarette advertising is disappearing on television. Equal time is given to antismoking commercials. The ads of the American Cancer Society, warning of the evils of smoking, are seen everywhere. An attempt is being made to educate the youth of America to the danger of cigarettes. Smoking is dangerous to your health. Tests have shown that the risk of lung cancer increases dramatically when you smoke. Some entertainers now refuse to permit advertisements for cigarettes on their shows. Others will not accept jobs as actors in smoking ads. The American tobacco industry took out a full-page ad in *The New York Times* condemning the *Times* for refusing to accept cigarette advertising that does not contain the disclaimer that smoking is bad for your health. We have the ironic situation of the tobacco industry's generating high employment in certain parts of the country, while at the same time that industry is condemned for destroying health.

The advertiser seems to say, "I exist only to serve my client. He gives me the facts about his product. I then seek to package it in an attractive way for the public. I am not a moralist. I am a businessman." Occasionally the government does step in. A certain soup manufacturer had been using marbles in its TV advertising, giving the impression that the soup had big chunks of tasty food in it. The company was told to stop such false promotion. They countered with the claim that to photograph the soup as it really was did not give a true impression of their product. They saw nothing wrong in using marbles as "props" to promote their soup.

At times the moral issue has been raised. False advertising that seeks to deceive has been roundly condemned. The store that advertises a product at a certain price, and then has only two or three of those items on the shelves, may be accused of fraudulent promotion. Outright fraud, such as weighted scales in a meat market or the watering down of high-test gasoline with low-test gasoline—is unlawful, and most would say such actions are immoral. What is not so certain is the "gray" area—the whole morality of whetting the public's taste for inferior products that will soon go out of style. In the film *The Graduate* the young man was told that the answer to life was plastics. He was advised that the best career would be in plastic products. They are fairly durable, can be easily molded, and quickly discarded. Records are made of plastic. Once the mold is cast, the record can be produced by the thousands, if not millions, at a very reasonable cost. As long as the record is in demand, it is no problem to make additional copies.

The advertiser declares that his work brightens up the world. He promotes products that people may never have imagined, but once they have them, they become necessities. The air-conditioning industry has made giant strides. It has shown people the way to more comfort. The luxury of yesterday becomes the necessity of today. At one time, women cooked their own vegetables. Now they can obtain them packaged, canned or frozen. The advertiser would argue that he has made life easier for the consumer and has generated new jobs in new industries at the same time. He might say that "built-in obsolescence" is good for the economy. So what if a TV picture tube goes bad the day after the ninety-day guarantee expires? Is it not good for the tube manufacturer to know that his product is in demand? So what if new cars are full of "bugs" and defects? After all, the auto mechanic has to make a living, too. What is wrong with a little shoddiness? One is reminded of the remark of one of the astronauts. He was asked what bothered him the most about space travel. He replied, "The fact that every item in the space capsule was built by the lowest bidder."

The pharmaceutical industry is in a battle with certain legislators. The fight has to do with whether brand-name drugs are really any better than generic products. The industry says its products are superior, having been developed and tested over a long period of time. They say further that they have invested many millions of dollars in each new drug that appears on the market. They feel they have a right to charge enough to get back a fair return on their investment, before some new pill is developed to replace the old one. Senate investigators have charged that abnormally high profits have been made on certain pills, and that these same pills, when not sold under a brand name, can be purchased for a fraction of the cost. Critics of the pharmaceutical industry have charged that brand-name products are often not carefully tested, that they can have dangerous side effects, and that far too many new products are being given to physicians to try on their patients. The battle rages in and out of the halls of Congress. Thoughtful persons have questioned the honesty and wisdom of much of the advertising for medicinal products. How ethical is it for a drug manufacturer to advertise that his product will sufficiently calm your nerves so that you can become president of the high-school class? Or when you are upset by your parents' nagging you about taking your little brother to the baseball game or dance, the same drug will calm your nerves. Much advertising is geared to the needs, anxieties, and worries of your generation. Salves to remove pimples and blotches are always in demand. New cure-alls for acne are promoted with gusto on the rock-and-roll radio stations. For the over-40 crowd, magic potions are available to rejuvenate your "tired blood." The old-fashioned medicine man of the early West is replaced by the modern advertiser who has a variety of products to peddle in your living room through the magic of color television.

Many millions of dollars have been invested in products of questionable value. Skilled lobbyists are constantly at work to persuade senators and congressmen not to investigate certain products of doubtful value. Reforms in automobile safety were largely the result of the courage of one man who single-handedly, with little financial support, fought the car manufacturers. Thanks to Ralph Nader's efforts, many new safety devices are now standard equipment on the new automobiles.

Industry will argue that too much policing will stifle the free market of goods. To be creative, industry must operate in an arena of freedom, with minimum controls. They might say, "What right has a federal agency to determine the chicken content of a frankfurter?" If the government feels the consumer is being deceived, then it would appear that false advertising must be stopped. The dishonest merchant operates on the premise, "Let the buyer beware." False claims are made for shoddy merchandise, which should arouse public protests.

False advertising and extravagant claims are unethical. That we know. But there is that semiethical area in which controversy exists. Are advertisers leading the public, or are they merely responding to wishes already present? Do the advertisers have too much to say in shaping the public taste? Are they the servants of the public, or its masters? Do they merely accent trends already present, or do they pioneer new ground that is harmful? Are fads overly exploited by industry? Are we moving into the credit-card age to such an extent that our teenagers are already overloaded with debts? Has society made it so easy for you to purchase goods on time that by the time you pay for them, they will be worn out and useless? Those are some of the ethical issues being raised in our consumer-credit economy. All segments of society are affected, not only the youth. The Puritan frugality of the past is largely dead. The question remains as to the ethical nature of living beyond one's means and never truly catching up with the bills that keep pouring in. Is it the responsibility of your parents to show you the wise use of money, or is there also a responsibility that should be exercised by the mass media not to overstimulate the buying public to go hopelessly into debt? Periods of inflation and high spending can give way to recession and even depression. It has happened before. Do we need some restraints? And if so, where should they originate?

Youth has organized for a variety of causes. To my knowledge, you have not created an organization to study the effect of advertising on you and your money. Would such a study be valuable? Could parents help? Adults do belong to consumer groups. Adults do become concerned when prices are too high. Women in Levittown, New York, went on a meat strike when they felt the price of beef was far out of line. A department of consumer affairs exists in Washington. Most large cities and counties have policing departments to look into fraudulent actions in the field of merchandising.

The larger question remains: How free can a "free" society remain? The young do not want restraints. Should industry be policed? Should industry be warned about built-in obsolescence? Should advertisers be restrained in promoting more and more credit spending? Ultimately, you will give the answer by how you spend the dollar you have in your pocket.

Influence of Television

Sociologists estimate that by the time you reach the age of 18, you will have spent 20,000 hours watching television. That is far more than you will have spent with your teachers in school. It may even rival the attention span you have utilized with your family and friends. America has become a nation of spectators. On a Sunday afternoon, you may find yourself spending your time watching a sports program, then take a break for dinner, and come back to the TV set for the evening shows. Alarmist articles have been written about the "Big Tube" that is converting us into a lazy nation of sitters and viewers. Instead of talking to friends, we watch celebrities talk to one another on the late-night "talk" shows. McLuhan's "hot" medium is a powerful influence.

What should be the role of television? Should it exist to entertain? Should it be a teaching machine? At present, the television industry is geared to popularity ratings. It seeks to give the viewers what they want. If violence causes the ratings to go up, then blood and gore will fill the tiny screen. If comedy shows are in, then the new season lineup will feature fun and canned laughter. If a hillbilly show succeeds, then the other networks will come up with carbon copies of the hit program. When widows and widowers with children "sell," then a host of similar productions are featured.

The question has been raised as to the ethics of television. From time to time, Congress has investigated the networks. Legislators have asked why there is so much violence in the prime time viewing periods. The TV industry is quick to respond, and for a time violence will subside. The blood-and-guts Western will be replaced by the cowboy hero who employs psychology and persuasion to overcome the villain. The TV networks are sensitive to governmental criticism. Their license renewals depend on favorable governmental action. TV stations are very profitable. The networks walk a tightrope between giving the public what it wants and appeasing those who agree with the former FCC chairman who labeled the fare on TV a "vast wasteland," with entertainment that is amusing at best and shoddy at worst. The production costs of shows have mounted to astronomical figures. When a guest star can receive $10,000 for a brief segment on a TV special, you know that much is at stake in the "ratings game." Heads of networks rise and fall according to who is ahead when the Nielsen surveys are published. The higher the ratings, the easier it becomes to sell time to the advertisers. Economics are such that shows survive because of popularity.

A debate has been raging as to the effects of television on the viewer. One reads in the newspapers of a young man who is arrested for committing a crime he says he modeled after a felony shown on TV. Educators bemoan the proliferation of violence on the small screen. They say it will influence youth to try the same techniques in a real-life situation. When national leaders such as President Kennedy and Martin Luther King were assassinated, voices were heard that claimed TV had created the climate of violence.

I spoke with a friend, a freshman at Northeastern College in Boston. I said, "Any excitement at your school?"

He replied, "S.D.S. created some excitement over the Vietnam issue. A meeting was held. S.D.S. occupied the interfaith rooms of the Student Union building. About 5,000 students and faculty gathered in the Quadrangle. For about a half hour there was fighting between S.D.S.'ers and a group of the school's physical education majors. While the fighting went on, the TV cameras were working and interviews were held. Then the scuffling stopped. For the next three to four hours anyone who wished to talk could do so. I stood next to a TV cameraman. As long as there was fighting, he pushed forward and the cameras were 'live.' When things became calm and the students stood motionless to listen to the speakers who represented different points of view, the cameras and microphones were turned off. I asked a TV newsman why he stopped the cameras now that things were quiet. He shrugged his shoulders. The heart of the day was the wonderful way in which the rioting subsided and a fine discussion was held by students who behaved well toward each other. This was of no interest to the Boston TV reporters. All they wanted was the 'violence' and 'hysteria.' The brief scuffle was built up into something much bigger than it was—at least for the home TV viewer." My college friend looked at me. "Was that right, what the TV people did?" He answered his own question, "I don't think so."

When the young see a lack of morality on the part of the mass media, they become disillusioned. The big story of TV was "violence" in living color. The real story was the wonderful way in which emotion and passion gave way to reasonableness. Each point of view was expressed. The mass of students remained in the Quadrangle to hear the arguments aired by both sides.

My friend continued, "It did not degenerate into the type of riot they had at Harvard. Cooler heads prevailed."

One wonders why constructive matters are so often overlooked. If conflict is the heart of the news, can we ever have peace in the world? The mass media can be a tremendous force for good. They certainly have dramatized the problems involved in the Vietnamese war. The war does not emerge as a glorious combat in most TV reports. The military and the government are less than happy about TV and press coverage of the Southeast Asian struggle. In their desire to get a dramatic story, only the dramatic elements—which means violence—are normally reported. A pacified village in which progress has been made is seldom seen by the home viewer. The village burned by napalm glows on the TV screen—and editorial judgment is passed on our actions by the reporter at the scene. Seldom do we get a report in any depth. There is always time for commercials. Seldom is there time for detailed reporting on matters of substance. The incident at Northeastern University is a case in point. The Boston stations played up the "sensational" elements in the story. What really happened was lost to the average Bostonian. The fact that the young people were able to overcome an initial scuffle and show respect for one another—that was not "news." Anyone can be good.

It may be that the new morality should call for more balanced reporting as to what is really going on in the world. If students at a college are to be judged on the basis of a brief scuffle, then that is unfair coverage. The moral approach would demand a total view and evaluation of any student disturbance. A chain reaction can set in when TV inflames the country by featuring only the violence. There is more to college life than the flare-ups on some campuses. If the quieter moments of introspection were recorded, more ultimate good would result. How can judgments be rendered without a consideration of all the factors?

The few who riot are on the evening TV news. The vast student body that behaves is forgotten. They are not newsworthy.

When race riots swept through Detroit, Watts, and other cities, TV was accused of fanning the flames that caused the long, hot summer of burning and lawlessness. People spoke of the "instant leader" who was created by TV. He was the man with the loudest voice, who threatened to burn down the cities unless his demands were met. The handling of the news has become a sensitive issue. Network newsmen are now somewhat more careful in covering riots. They fear a chain reaction, whereby viewers in other cities are inspired to cause riots by what they see happening elsewhere. What is legitimate news coverage? How much TV time should be given to the extremists who say, "Burn, baby, burn"? When the college campuses have erupted with sit-ins and demonstrations, the TV reporter is near at hand with camera and microphone. In this age of "instant journalism" and the creation of "instant leaders" because of wide TV coverage, we see that moral and ethical questions do arise.

The TV handling of the Chicago Democratic Convention in 1968 raised anew the problem of the power of TV. Mayor Richard Daley of Chicago emerged as a TV villain who manipulated the convention, while outside the halls young students had their heads bloodied by the police. TV cameras would focus for a moment on the dais, where a speaker would extoll the virtues of the Democratic Party and its struggle to grant equality to minorities, and then, almost in the next instant, the cameras would focus on the student demonstrators being herded into police wagons as they were dragged screaming and bloody from the streets near the convention hall. The visual image has a tremendous impact. It generates excitement. It causes bitter debate. Should television be somehow regulated and brought under governmental control? Does it foster disunity in America? Is it an instrument of the devil, or the best example of democracy in action?

Authorities are not in agreement about the effects of TV on

the viewer. One school of thought holds that violence on TV provides a harmless release. It is a good way to vent one's emotions. By vicariously sharing in a violent Western, we expend our hostilities in a harmless way, and are thus not as likely to go out and do violence to others. A different point of view would hold that violence on TV serves to stimulate borderline psychotics and neurotics to actually go out and perform their terrible fantasies. Does TV act to trigger potential criminals to acts of terror, or is it more likely to be a healthy release for thoughts of aggression? All of the evidence is not in. The debate is far from settled. Meanwhile, the networks keep a wary eye on the barometers of public sentiment. TV dislikes governmental investigation and censure. It is an industry that must work hard at winning friends and projecting a good public image.

Does democracy impose limits? Is it ethical for a newscaster to tell a group of demonstrators to start waving their posters and screaming for the cameras? Are staged demonstrations— to help build up ratings—ever justified? The TV newsman might say that he is bringing the attention of the public to the vital problems of our day. Can anyone really say whether a particular program will incite to violence and lead to a threat to our way of life? Should anarchists who advocate the violent overthrow of a university be featured on TV news or documentary programs? Who is ultimately to judge what is newsworthy and what is not?

Actually we have two separate problems, although they are related. One concerns the fictional violence of the TV dramatic show. The other concerns the actual violence of the real world. The networks have begun to recognize that in fiction shows, too much blood and gore bring censure. However, the problem of violence in life—as it occurs on the streets of our cities—is in a different category. A newsman may feel that he has to present whatever is newsworthy, whether it is pleasant or unpleasant. He will resent self-censorship and feel that his judgment should be his alone, and not the judgment of some self-appointed moralizer. Good deeds seldom make the headlines. Wars, crimes of passion, dissent—those are the rubrics of the public taste. The mass media are geared to the sensational statement or program. Action groups have discovered that quiet discussions seldom produce results. The student leaders at Columbia, who led the demonstrations there, were quick to point out that pleas through legitimate channels had been fruitless. Confrontation seems to be the best way to achieve results. The civil rights movement moved forward as the TV cameras watched. When the police unleashed dogs on peaceful demonstrators, America uttered a collective gasp. The public is affected by television coverage of fast-breaking events.

Television has great power to shape public attitudes. A photogenic candidate for high office can be helped by televised appearances. It has been said that Richard Nixon lost his first bid for the White House because he did poorly in the TV debates with John Kennedy. It was charged that Nixon's makeup man purposely failed to make him up properly; so that he appeared sallow and heavy bearded on the screen. It was charged that the makeup man was a Democrat.

The TV industry has pointed to the growing number of educational channels that provide instruction rather than pure entertainment. In actuality, the educational networks cry that they lack funds to perform adequately for the public. It often seems, when watching the educational channels, that they spend as much time on their personal commercials begging for funds, as the commercial channels do with their overload of advertising messages. Critics of the industry have said that commercial TV is not anxious for educational outlets to become too successful, lest too many viewers be enticed away from the entertainment channels.

Television producers seek to give the public what it wants. If the young want a less violent product, that is what you will get. The industry is responsive to trends and viewer tastes. Letters to the networks are read and tabulated. Should the TV industry work to raise the cultural level of the viewers, or should the industry continue to cater to the basic tastes of those who watch? At the moment, the latter approach dominates.

The TV industry reflects the changing mores of America. Networks now give greater freedom to comedians. Jokes once considered off-color are not "beeped out" as frequently. Skillful writers now manage to get double-meaning remarks on the airwaves. The comedians will say that each viewer will get out of the joke whatever he sees in it. Political satire is seldom censured. Impressionists who impersonate our national leaders— from the President on down—find wide viewer acceptance. The one area of sensitivity that remains is that of religious satire. Satirical barbs against the religious sensibilities of viewers are often the basis of argument. The comic who mocks God will not find an audience on TV. The "blue" comedian whose routine is peppered with too many off-color stories will remain in the nightclub, unless he can clean up or modify his material for a TV guest appearance. The TV industry hopes to remain basically self-policing. Does censorship become necessary when self-policing seems to fail? How much freedom should this giant be allowed to have?

Panel discussions are now held on homosexuality, abortion, premarital intercourse, and wife swapping. A few years ago, such discussions would have been taboo. Greater openness and freedom prevail. TV tries to "tell it like it is," and still retain its freedom from excessive censorship. What TV says will more and more reflect the interests, tastes, and desires of youth. Teenagers make up a significant portion of the viewing audience. Is TV immoral? Few teenagers have raised moral objections to the material presented.

Censorship of Television?

Much is certainly wrong with television. Its news coverage is often unbalanced. As viewers, we may not approve of the emphasis given to certain stories. The Nixon administration has shown great sensitivity over the coverage given to speeches by administration officials. It has condemned the networks for instant commentary on a major presidential policy address. The chairman of the FCC asked for transcripts of the comments made by commentators concerning a presidential address on Vietnam. Many were angered over actions that seemed to indicate a move toward censorship of television news.

The moral question arises, since the following could happen: A commentator criticizes government policy. The owners of the network are warned that the news was slanted. The commentator persists in expressing his thoughts. The station finds its license may not be renewed. It is accused of not serving the public interest in a fair and impartial way. This is a problem that needs to be resolved. Freedom to act is the right of the news media, be it television, radio, or the press. Reporters are looking for a story. Dramatic events attract viewers. Should television only reflect the mood of most Americans? Does it have a role to challenge and goad public officials? Is the medium true to itself if it becomes a mirror for the dissemination of what a government official thinks is good for us? Harry Truman said, "If you can't stand the heat, then get out of the kitchen." To be in politics means that you are constantly subjected to all sorts of criticism. In a democracy, vigorous dissent, discussion, and debate are eternal. Feelings are hurt. Policy statements are misinterpreted. The TV viewer may be shown only an extract from an important speech. What the speaker sought to emphasize may never be shown on camera. Electronic journalism creates instant public response. The accusation has been made that control of what is or is not news rests in the hands of a few commentators in the East—in New York and Washington. Forty million viewers are thus given only a biased view of what is or is not news. That is the accusation one hears.

So, we do have a moral issue. Who shall decide what goes on the airwaves? Should programming be done by the professional commentators, with many years of experience in the newsgathering business? Or should there be a panel of concerned citizens to lend guidance to the networks, so as to broaden the scope and base of the news? It has been charged that the Easterners possess a liberal bias, and do not truly reflect the interests and tastes of the broad spectrum of middle America. We have heard the term the "silent majority." It refers to the vast bulk of Americans who do not protest or speak out—yet they have thoughts, ideas, feelings, and they are basically patriotic and tend to support whoever is in the White House. The charge is heard that the group is being manipulated and brainwashed by sinister eastern broadcasters who reflect only the liberal view on major issues. Critics of the networks would hold that more time and coverage are given to peace marchers than to loyalty-day parades.

The morality of conduct by TV reporters is suspect. The networks reply that they must be given the freedom to "tell it like it is." They hold that in a democracy you cannot censure the mass media—it would be the end of democracy as we know it. To hold the sword of Damocles over the broadcaster's head would mean that we are fast becoming a police state in which thought control, à la George Orwell's *1984,* would become a grim reality. The specter of fascism and Nazism are before us. In Czechoslovakia the "spring of freedom" gave way to the winter of censorship and harsh repression. Critics of administration attacks on broadcasters now shriek with alarm. Censorship is on the way, as the government moves against those who are in opposition.

Those who support the administration say that they are truly moral. They claim that for too long TV has not been fair to the government—especially in its handling of the war in Vietnam. Is it moral to condemn the President for not ending the conflict swiftly enough? Let us give the new President a chance to end the war with American honor still intact. Let us stress what is good about American foreign policy, and not what is wrong with it. We shall destroy the foundations of American democracy if we lose all sense of patriotic values and virtues. Anarchy, rioting, and revolution are simmering below the surface. Those dark forces are unleashed and encouraged by irresponsible broadcasters who seek only the sensational story—to the detriment of American democracy. American foreign policy cannot be made in the streets. Marches and demonstrations do not truly reflect what most Americans are thinking. In November of 1969 those who supported the President drove with their headlights on during the daylight hours, in silent protest against the more vocal marchers who went to Washington the weekend of November 15.

The following arguments were heard: Give the President the chance to win an honorable peace in Paris. Do not give aid and comfort to the enemy. Forty thousand American soldiers have died in Vietnam. Keep faith with our dead by giving us the time to withdraw from Southeast Asia with honor. It would be immoral to permit our war dead to have died in vain. America has never lost a war. Dissent at home may cause us to leave Vietnam in disgrace. We face rioting and anger at home if we lose the war. Support the President so that he can end the war without America losing face. All of Asia may fall to communism if we fail to stand firm. Critics of the war are immoral. Those who unfairly criticize our government are traitors.

So we have a clash of views. Each side claims that it is moral and the other is immoral. The lessons of the past are instructive. In the 1950's America experienced an era of McCarthyism. People were afraid to speak, for fear of being branded as Communists. Conformity was the order of the day. People were summarily dismissed from government jobs because they were suspected of being Communists. The era of McCarthyism finally passed. It was a product of a slight recession and the Korean conflict. The late Senator Joseph McCarthy appealed to the prejudices and fears of many Americans. The majority breathed a sigh of relief when his era ended. The late Ed Morrow of CBS had the courage to confront and challenge Senator McCarthy. Others followed suit. Public opinion changed. McCarthyism faded.

In our own time there are those who clamor for a more

responsible type of reporting and coverage. Many of their complaints are justified. But we must be careful not to move from responsible criticism to outright repression and the engendering of fear.

Motion Pictures

The new freedom and permissiveness are nowhere more evident than in the films being shown today. Simulation of the act of sexual intercourse is permitted. The showing of the actual act of coitus on the screen is considered pornographic. As long as a film has some redeeming social significance, explicit sex is allowed. Nudity has become common. A few years ago, a fleeting glimpse of a woman's breast was considered daring. Today, extended close-ups of couples in bed—in the act of simulated coitus—are becoming almost standard. As long as nudity and coitus serve to advance the plot in a film with some social message, it can be shown. Homosexuality is treated with a degree of frankness. Boys embrace boys. Girls embrace girls. The sex act involving multiple partners has become a subject for films.

The Hays office is no more. The office was sponsored by the film industry to examine all motion pictures as to fitness for viewing. Explicit sex was forbidden by the Hays office. Hollywood does little to police itself. Foreign films stress nudity. The home-grown film product has to be more sexually oriented to compete with the foreign imports. The censorship laws are interpreted in a very liberal manner. Anything short of outright pornography is shown. Some states police and censure films. By and large, very little is deleted from the screen. The "x" rating, which forbids those under 17 from entering the theater, does not deter the viewing public. Quite to the contrary. The "x"-rated film may be doing the best business in town! *I Am Curious (Yellow)* has been a phenomenal success. The low-budget sex-oriented movie can have a wide viewing public.

Filmmaking is now an attractive career for young people. Young filmmakers are found everywhere in our major cities.

Experimentation in films as the newest art form is seen everywhere. Almost complete freedom holds sway. Andy Warhol did not run into serious censorship problems until he filmed his "blue" movie, which showed the actual act of sexual intercourse. A couple discussed the morality of the Vietnamese war as they engaged in coitus. The New York law officers did not consider the movie to have sufficient redeeming social significance. At this writing, the matter is being tried in the courts. The last word from the courts has not yet been spoken. Coitus may actually be permitted on the screen. The sex organs can be photographed freely in films—as is the case in *I Am Curious (Yellow)*.

Even as TV has come under critical fire for being immoral in its presentation of violence, so has the film industry been severely taken to task for the proliferation of nudity and sexuality. Critics of films hold that sex has been sensationalized. The term "sexploitation" has been used to describe the promotion efforts of the filmmakers. Some politicians sense a public revulsion against excessive nudity on film, and now promise if elected to clean up their city, as they solemnly pledge to declare war on the smut purveyors who corrupt the moral sensibilities and feelings of the theatergoing public. Fundamentalist preachers inveigh against the growing open purveying of movies that blatantly promote bizarre sexuality. Public officials are urged to control and police the motion picture theaters where such films are exhibited.

Filmmakers argue that they should be free to do anything they wish. The public is the ultimate arbiter of what succeeds or fails. They say they are expressing their own integrity and courage in filmmaking. The imposition of restraints is bitterly resented. Theaters do rate films, and an effort is made to keep those under 17 or 18 out of theaters showing films rated "x." The film industry has liberalized its standards—in keeping with the greater sexual freedom that is found in our society. Films do indeed reflect the interests, attitudes, prejudices, and desires of the public. If there is public approval and acceptance of more nudity, then nudity will be shown. If the public tires of overt sexuality in films, then filmmakers will respond with a different stance. Some speak of a "sexual overkill" in films and say that the public will tire of the excessive nudity. They say that sex alone will not sell the newer films. Crowds will flock to a good picture with sexuality, and they will avoid a poor picture with sexuality, in the opinion of some filmmakers and critics. Once the novelty of simulated coitus on the screen wears off, films will have to be more than sexually stimulating to attract the crowds. That may prove to be the end result of sexual freedom in motion pictures.

While filmmakers argue for freedom, the critics clamor for realistic standards. Those who look in horror at the ads for films are convinced that movies now create a climate of overly permissive conduct. The sexual moralist believes that there is no one to promote his cause. He feels that the message of sexual freedom is the message that is constantly before the public. His attitudes are not heard. Not all those who oppose sexuality in films belong to the extremist fringe of society. Many thoughtful educators and clergymen are concerned that a subject as personal and as sacred as love—and the act of love—should be so blatantly advertised and presented. They feel that a threat to the sanctity of the American home arises when sexual promiscuity involving extramarital affairs is sympathetically portrayed. If the unfaithful wife or husband emerges as a hero in films, what will our youth think? So some are concerned lest the institution of marriage itself, already beset with a host of difficulties in our high-divorce-rate culture, sustain yet further blows as a result of the new sex models on the screen. Psychologists tell us that we need models after whom we tend to fashion our lives. If the sex adventurer becomes the model, then some see a danger to the stability of society.

Should teenagers be allowed to see any film that is shown in a theater? Does one need a certain level of maturity before he should be allowed to view a certain type of film? At the moment, theaters do exclude teenagers from the "x"-rated film, and the "m"- or "r"-rated film may or may not be seen by them.

Is there something to be said for a youth's not being allowed to see a particular film? What about the concept of "pleasure delayed"? Must every desire be gratified at once? Are there still areas in which it might be wiser to wait?

Some parents honestly prefer to have the films rated. In that way the decision is already made for them. A film is a blind item. You do not know what it is until you see it. Some "M" and "R" films are innocuous; others are not. Some films are purposely rated "M" or "R" to stimulate interest. Their sexuality may be minimal.

As with TV, some question exists as to whether sexuality in films is a healthy release for a viewer or acts as a stimulant to the violation of accepted moral codes. Experts on both sides of the argument can be cited. In the Scandinavian countries where censorship is minimal, interest in pornography has declined. It may be that the new freedom in films will give way to new boredom. Only time and the public taste can tell.

Books and Magazines

I discussed with a friend the problem of what teenagers were reading. He said, "One day I called my son in and said, 'Here is a copy of *Playboy* magazine.' The boy was amazed. 'Do you really want me to have it?' he said in a hesitant voice. He took the magazine. Now he spends less time at the magazine rack of the local candy store." To read or not to read certain books and magazines—that becomes a question. As a youth, you are curious to read and to see literature and pictures that society may consider improper. Parents try to set rules. You may wonder why.

First, let us ask what motivates your parents. Basically, they are interested in your proper development. They are not anxious for you to read any books or magazines that might be harmful to your emotional growth. Some psychologists hold that definite negative development can result if you fill your mind with pornographic literature. It is natural for a parent to wish to protect his offspring. "Clean thoughts in a clean mind" is a primary consideration of the adult world. If parents seek to limit or censure your reading habits, they do so out of genuine concern— not because they wish to wield authority. The point is, your parents do care about you. They are concerned that pornography will give you ideas and motivate you to act in a way that you are not prepared to handle. In New York City are to be found "peep show" bookstores. Youths under 18 are not allowed to enter. Material that many would consider to be hard-core pornography is sold in such places. In addition, unsavory individuals may frequent the "girly" bookstore, looking for young boys and girls to share in some action of a more dramatic nature than just reading a pornographic magazine. As a youth, you feel that you can handle yourself in any situation. You may resent it when parents say, "Stay away from that bookstore. You will never know what trouble you can find there." Parents do not act out of malice. Maximum freedom is provided by most adults for their children. However, they can see certain dangers. We should not cross the street against a red light. That is a good law: it can save your life. Certain sections of your city may be unsafe. A parent will set limits.

What do some parents do? As mentioned earlier, they may have some books and magazines in the home for you to read. They may prefer that you read them in your own home, rather than going elsewhere to seek visual excitement. Others may be rather stern about having such literature in your room, and they may object violently to your sneaking such things into the house.

Youthful reaction to censorship is resentment. A typical attitude is "I should be allowed to read or to see anything." Yet your reaction to parental rules—be they strict or liberal—will ultimately depend on the degree of confidence and trust that you have established with your parents. If you have a good relationship with them—if you are free and open in your discussion of many things (and not just sexuality)—then the procedure involving reading material will be worked out in terms of mutual satisfaction. Do your parents have confidence in you?

Do you trust their judgment? How do you regard one another in the process of growing toward adulthood? Those bigger questions can provide more basic answers to the immediate everyday crises in family life.

Parents function in a world that is confusing and largely without enforceable codes and standards. In this day and age, censorship has been eliminated for most books and magazines. In New York City, magazines that have been labeled hardcore pornography are sold openly. They have no redeeming social value. The police would like to ban such publications from the newsstands. Periodically, a clergyman or an irate citizen will declaim against such magazines before the TV cameras. A brief crackdown may ensue. Soon the magazines reappear. We do live in times of greater freedom. America at this stage has moved in the direction of greater liberality. Articles appear that praise the Scandinavian attitude of little or no censorship. We are told that countries with few rules against pornography soon discover that pornography tends to go out of style; in one Scandinavian country, the booksellers complained that only the tourists were buying their pornographic products. As one put it, "Only really good pornography is being bought." One wonders what "good" pornography might be?

America has a vestige of the pioneer spirit. The pioneer who went West was a free man, defending his home. He made his own laws. At the same time, the pioneer did subscribe to some of the Puritan virtues. Cleanliness of mind and purity of heart were cherished values. Today, Americans are torn between the desire to be free, open, and uncensored and, on the other hand, not to lose the heritage of Puritan standards of decency and modesty. It is no wonder adults have trouble in determining how to act.

Some parents who have brought pornography into the home have been astonished to discover that their own children resented such actions. "What would my friends say, if they found out that my parents are reading that kind of magazine?" The excitement of discovery and adventure is gone when the parent brings the offensive material into the living room. At that point, you may realize how little such "literature" is really worth. Is there a solution to the matter? Possibly if the parent and child sat down with the book or magazine and read it together, and then discussed it, clarification and a better feeling would be engendered. At least, you would not feel guilty if mother found an offending magazine while cleaning out your dresser drawers. Not every parent wants to discuss such a magazine with you. They may be too embarrassed to do so. Such discussions do not come naturally to many parents. That is why sex education in the schools can be so helpful. It will aid you to develop attitudes and strengthen you in the area of understanding. A little bit of knowledge can clear the air. With greater knowledge of sexuality, you can take the so-called "dirty" books in your stride.

Authorities are divided on the question as to whether erotic desire is created by pornographic material. Some hold that it is merely a healthy outlet for sexual feelings. Others are quick to point out that it can trigger unacceptable social action. When the sex deviate is apprehended after a crime, his room will often be found to be crammed with erotic literature. Is it the fault of the literature, the individual, or society when a sex crime is committed? No agreement exists on the issue—even as there is no firm agreement that violence on television will affect the crime rate in the streets. In September of 1969 the National Commission on Violence issued a report saying that TV programs contribute to violence in America. In an eleven-page report, they said, "In a fundamental way, television helps to create a picture of what children expect of themselves and of others, and of what constitutes the standards of civilized society. Yet . . . we daily permit our children during their formative years to enter a world of police interrogations, of gangsters beating enemies, of spies performing fatal brain surgery, and of routine demonstrations of all kinds of killing and maiming" (*Newsday*, Sept. 25, 1969). The report dealt harshly with parents who use TV as a babysitter, not caring what their children are watching. The same criticism could be leveled at parents who permit their youngsters to read and possess erotic literature. "At least the kid is reading something." The Commission report condemns the fact that both "good guys" and "bad guys" use violence to solve problems and achieve goals. They seem to be calling for a moral ethic to guide the TV producers. That same desire for a moral ethic motivates those who call for greater censorship of books and magazines. They would hold that unless society gives the parents support in the area of smut control, all is lost.

Greater freedom from censorship certainly imposes more problems on both parents and children. As the courts hand down lenient decisions in pornography cases, the burden is shifted to the parent and the child. Decisions will be made in the home. Attitudes will develop at the family hearth. If permissiveness continues to be the pattern, families may find it almost impossible to swim against the tide. Already we hear voices saying that all censorship of books and magazines should be abolished. They argue that if pornography is openly sold, it will lose its attractiveness.

In addition to the newsstand sale of pornography, we have the continuing legal battle involving material sent through the mails. The post office receives indignant letters from individuals who receive unsolicited pornographic materials. They argue that no one has the right to send such advertisements and pictures to their homes. They consider it an invasion of privacy. Voices are being raised against those offenders who mail the homeowner ads for materials of an obscene nature. Is it an improper use of the mails? Once again, the courts seem to vacillate. At times, a publisher is jailed; at other times, he goes free. The principle of artistry or redeeming social value can be open to interpretation. A parent says, "I would hate to have my child open such a piece of unsolicited mail. They have no right to send such trash to my home. I did not ask to be on their mailing list." Everyone receives a great deal of unsolicited mail. We seldom object. Pornography, unasked for, is something else again. It does provoke strong reactions.

Does anything really shock the teenager in today's world? The war in Vietnam is played out in living color each night on the TV screen. The news reports speak of unspeakable violence and rioting. Those who oppose censorship would hold that we have become unshockable and insensitive to visual impressions. They would say it is better to remove most restraints, since what is forbidden is not all that shocking or harmful. The real world is more of a shock and a horror than the fantasy world of the pornographer. Youth wants to know. Parents are concerned not so much as to how much you learn, but the way in which it is presented. Parents feel you are shockable and impressionable. You may feel otherwise.

Who Is to Blame?

Is the shift toward a sexually free and more open society the fault of the communications media—or is it a response to a more honest approach demanded by the public? TV producers keep their eyes glued to the ratings. If violence sells, then violence is in. If sex on TV aids the ratings of a show (and we see that more and more double-meaning jokes and sexy situations are portrayed), then sex is in. If booksellers discover that every best seller must have explicit sex descriptions, then authors will get the word as to what is required. If lurid tales and sensationalism are needed to stimulate magazine sales, then those, too, are likely to appear. We have a chain reaction. One TV program manages to include some questionable material. Their ratings soar. Soon a flock of others are using the same approach. Who is to blame? No one seems to know.

TV producers have discovered that educational programs cannot obtain sponsors. Entertainment shows that are not controversial command the best ratings. Authors have learned that explicit sex can lead to greater sales and a chance at the best-seller list. Films that are rated "G" (for general audience) may find few viewers. Without enforceable laws and standards, almost total freedom is the order of the day. It is difficult to blame the communications media. Self-policing of the TV or motion picture or book and magazine industry is an impossibility. Defenders of the mass media would say that every man should be free to do his own thing. Reflecting the independent attitudes of youth, they would say that adults are too fearful and conservative. Many of the new-wave moviemakers and authors are themselves rather young. They feel they have the pulse of youth. They know what youth wants. It would seem that the older generation is coming along the same path, but more slowly. Movie and theater critics will confess that although they may not like a certain film or play, the young audience was enthralled by the performance. Is there a growing distance between the standards of the young and the old? Is it far more than taste in music and in manner of dress and hair styles? Is there a whole new morality growing up around doing your own thing—honestly, openly, and without fear? Does an event such as the Woodstock Music Festival, where over 250,000 youths gathered for music—and for drugs—offer a preview of a new youth culture that is becoming normal for a growing minority of young people today?

Adults have experience on their side. They have lived through the adventure and experimentation period of youth. They want only what they feel is good for the younger generation. They seek to guide. Some will demand. There is a legitimate fear that the new morality will lead to a breakdown of respect for authority in all fields—not just in the field of moral codes. They wonder if the young are not being used to enrich the bank accounts of peddlers of pornography. Is it right for you to be used by others? Is it your decision whether or not to buy or accept the wares of the marketplace? Do the parents have a duty to demand that the authorities create laws to protect you from harm? Are censorship laws against poisoning the mind in the same category as laws against selling tainted meat in a supermarket? Is the mind really being poisoned or just amused? The damage from tainted meat is readily seen. You may have to have your stomach pumped out! The effects of violence and sex in the mass media are not as measurable. Their total impact is still in question. So long as all the evidence is not in, what should society do? Are more laws needed? Must we listen to the public clamor to "clean up filth"?

Today, permissiveness holds sway in the mass media. Few books are left on the "reserved" shelf in the library, where they can be checked out only with parental consent. Availability— and "make up your own mind"—is what is seen and heard and practiced. You are under pressure to make your own decisions. You want a minimum of parental and adult authority. You seek participatory democracy, both at home and in your schools —and on the streets with your friends. You wish to see and experience much of what the world has to offer. Your parents may feel you are not quite ready to see and to do everything. What are the limits of behavior? Where does parental authority end, and the authority of your friends begin? Can and should lines of authority be established? Who should have the last word as to what you see, read, or do?

Parents seek to impose restraints. They say "wait." Society still urges modesty in sexual matters. The lurid magazine is read in secret. The girly bookstore is not considered a legitimate business. Hard-core pornography has not gained respectability as an art form.

When all is said and done, I wonder if you and your parents are really far apart in the matter of standards. If a youth can still be embarrassed by seeing his parents reading pornography at home, then it may be that your generation is not too different from that of your parents. The new morality may just be a new way of restating the older values. Does your new morality mean that you want complete freedom of choice in everything? Or do you seek a middle ground in which communication between the generations is desirable and regular?

Do you want your parents to agree with you most of the time? One teenager remarked to me, "My dad is no fun. He always agrees with me. If we have a discussion on the generation gap, he says 'Son, you're right.' " This youth was saying that he needed an authority to react against.

The young want adults to be honest. They can often detect the phony who uses youth to sell a product or to promote an idea. No one wishes to be exploited. The teenage market in goods and services is growing. The teenage dollar has vast purchasing power. The teenager is an important consumer. You are in danger of being used and exploited, on the theory that you will buy the sensational item—regardless of its value.

They tell the story of a wise man who stood before a king. The king said, "I am holding a bird in my hand. Tell me if the bird is alive or dead."

The wise man knew that if he said the bird was dead, the king would release it. If he said the bird was alive, the king would crush it. He thought for a moment and said, "Oh king, the fate of the bird is in your hand."

The fate of a TV show may depend on you. With a flick of the dial you can turn a program off. The future of the film producer depends on his appeal to youth. A picture that does not sell is worthless. A rock group that cannot sell its recordings is soon forgotten. "Youth power" is a fact. You are an economic factor in the spending of many millions—if not billions of dollars. The moral direction of the media is, to a great extent, in your hands.

CHAPTER VI

The Drug Scene

The teenager is influenced by his friends. You may have heard the following: "In our crowd, everyone smokes pot. If I don't smoke pot, then I won't have any friends."

Or: "There was this crowd I wanted to go with. Someone gave me some powdered stuff to try. I didn't know what it was. At first I felt dizzy. Later I felt good. I don't really like drugs. I am not sure what I was taking. But I have to follow the gang, or I won't have any friends."

A teenager speaks with great emotion: "Last year the kids were smoking marijuana. This year they're on 'hash.' The government has burned the fields. They can't get pot, so they're going for stronger stuff." When an adult asks a youth about pot, the answers are usually vague. You do not want to discuss it with your parents. Pot has become something that belongs to the young generation. Many have tried it. Some smoke it regularly. An attractive young person told me, "I usually smoke pot on the weekends. I am an artist. I find it helps me in my work. Sometimes I smoke pot by myself. At other times, I smoke with a crowd. Lately, my parents have become upset. I told them I will try to stop using it. Frankly, I cannot see what is wrong with pot. My parents smoke cigarettes. They have a cocktail before dinner. Smoking causes lung cancer. Alcohol can ruin your liver. There's no proof that pot harms you. All I get is a mild 'high.' "

Those of the young who have turned to chemicals as a way to "drop out" are not usually condemned by other young people. You seem to be saying, "If chemicals help, then let them use chemicals. My mom takes pep pills when she is low, and de-

110

pressants when she is high. My dad uses pills to stay awake to complete his work at the office. Adults use pills. Pills are pushed on TV and in the press. They are 'chemicals.' If my parents turn on with pep pills, why can't I find my own way to turn on? Amphetamines, barbiturates, opium, heroin—what's the difference? Besides, marijuana is not addicting, and liquor is more damaging to your health than pot."

Many adults feel that pot is but the first step to more potent drugs. They feel that the pushers are immoral, in that they are getting young people started on the road to destruction.

Marijuana—Harmless or Harmful?

Studies have been made as to why young people smoke pot. The following are some of the reasons: "It is the thing to do. Everyone was trying it. We got in a circle. Someone passed a joint around. If I didn't take a puff, I would not have been part of the crowd." You need to belong to a group. Few are "loners." Some fall into a crowd in which using pot is as normal as cigarette smoking or beer drinking.

Some turn to drugs for a new thrill. A teenager with his own car, a willing girl friend, money in his pocket, and free time is potentially a "pothead." He has tried everything. Why not smoke some "grass"?

Often teenagers are confused as to what parents expect of them. "My parents do not object if I take a drink. I can even smoke cigarettes at home. But if they knew I was on pot, would they get mad!" The forbidden is often the most inviting. Pot is one sure way to get a reaction from parents. Some teenagers crave attention. Pot is not something that parents can ignore. It is certainly a means to get a parent to sit down and talk with you.

All of us look for a model—the person we most admire. If the high-school hero is a pot smoker, others may join in the circle. On some campuses pot is very much the "in" thing. "The campus leaders all smoke it, why shouldn't I?"

"It's the cool thing to do." For the older teenager and for the youth on campus, the word "cool" connotes a mysterious something that the young strive to possess. If pot is "cool"— and impresses the opposite sex—then it becomes very desirable. A young man goes to a party. He asks a girl to go for a walk. She says, "Hey, I think I'm high." He is tempted to join her in smoking if he finds her attractive and desirable.

"Pot is exciting because it is illegal." If a raid has taken place at a high school, word of pot use spreads. It then becomes a daring feat to smoke it and not get caught. So, there is the added thrill of trying the forbidden. The cops represent the older generation who are spoiling the fun of the young people. It becomes a game. "Let's have a drag in secret and see if they catch us." Drug raids seem to make its use more popular on some campuses. The pot user then becomes somewhat of a celebrity. He has defied the Establishment. Even if he is caught and arrested, he may swagger with bravado: "Yeah, I spent the night in jail. Boy, were my folks mad!"

"I smoke pot because it is an escape. Youth cannot affect what is happening in the world. The older generation runs things. We are helpless." Some pot users have given up on struggling to succeed in changing the world. It is a way to "cop out." By contrast, a teenager I talked to was involved in an exciting project: "At our school they are letting us participate in a peace demonstration against the war in Vietnam. Most classes will go on. But during the day there will be special discussion groups held on the cause and meaning of the war. Those against the war, and those for it, will have a chance to speak. We are busy making signs and posters. It should be a really great day!" The girl who spoke had a sparkle in her eye. She is a young person who is very active in her Temple Youth group. She is an assistant teacher in religious school on Sunday morning. She has loads of friends of both sexes. She leads a very full life. She has not tried pot. Her world is a busy place. She is vivacious and constantly on the go. She cares about world and local problems. She does not believe that pot is a "with it" thing to take.

So, not all think and act the same way. "If there is pot smoking at a party, I will leave. I don't want to get arrested. I want to go to law school some day. With an arrest record, my whole future is in danger. I will not take such a chance. As long as pot is illegal, I will avoid it, and I will stay away from the pot smokers."

"I can find better things to do with my time than taking drugs. There is a political campaign in our town. The candidates are asking the youth to work for them. I will talk to the candidates and see if I can find the man who stands for the right ideals. Good politics means good government. I have other things to do than to take drugs. Who needs pot?"

Marijuana smoking is a retreat for some. It is a way to avoid responsibility. Parents bugging you? Escape with "grass." Doing poorly in school? Have a pot party. Get some recognition quickly! Some are avoiding reality. Pot is a way to delay facing problems. "My parents never let up on me. They don't come right out and say it, but I know they expect me to get all A's. I try the best I can. My teachers aren't that good. Some of them don't really teach that well. I'm not sure what my teachers expect from me. I do know that the report card is darn important to my parents. Frankly, I couldn't care less. Well, maybe I do care. I guess I do care about marks. But, to make high grades I spend all my time studying. But suppose I don't score high on the test? What will happen if I don't get into a good college? How will I feel? How will my folks feel? I often wonder if it's all worth it. Maybe I should just relax and light up a joint. The world goes on. The hip kids look happy and satisfied."

We cannot deny that the young exist in a pressure-filled world. Adults, too, are under pressure. Fathers work hard to provide comforts for the family. Some 30 percent or more of the mothers in America have full- or part-time jobs. Inflation eats into the family budget. The struggle to keep one's head above water— to meet mortgage payments, and just to stay ahead of the bills— is of real concern to the adult generation. As a youth, you can sense the tension. Your parents may not be around as often as you wish. Or you may wish they were around you even less, because discussions deteriorate into arguments: "I can't understand it. I can't even talk to my father. He doesn't discuss things. He only barks at me. We never talk. He only gives orders. He never talks to me, unless it is to ask me to do chores. All he has said to me in days is, 'Have you taken out the garbage and helped Mom with the dishes?' "

"I feel I'm the family scapegoat. Dad comes home upset. He takes it out on Mom. She yells at my older sister. My sister then yells at me. Our house is usually in an uproar. The only peace I find is to go out with the guys and sneak a joint behind the candy store. If I ever get caught, I'll never hear the end of it."

Parents also feel helpless and trapped: "I smelled a sweet smell in his room. He told me it was incense. He swore it wasn't pot. I really don't know what pot is. I did not want to question him too closely. Kids these days are funny. Everything is a private matter. They hardly ever talk to you, unless they need money. I cannot understand my teenage son. I wonder what's going on in his mind. We are generous parents. He never lacks for money, clothes, and the use of the family car."

"I don't know why my daughter smokes pot with her friends. I worry about her. Maybe she will try other drugs that are more harmful. When I was her age we smoked cigarettes and took an occasional drink. Drugs were nowhere to be found. Could it be that now that cigarettes are proven harmful to health, the kids are turning to marijuana—where the evidence is not in, as yet, as to its harmful effects?"

Another adult comments: "Each generation has to do its own thing. The kids today have taken to pot. This is their 'thing.' The best way to get them to stop would be for adults to start smoking grass. Boy, would that shake them up! But then they'd look for something else to try. Maybe adult pot smoking isn't such a good idea after all."

Who Smokes Pot?

At one time the majority of users were found in two principal groups: the underprivileged and the overprivileged. The first group consists of those living in the slums of our cities. They exist in what has been termed a drug culture. "I walk out on the street and I see the pusher. He is my friend. He drives a big car. He sells me enough stuff for a few joints. Some look down on him. I feel he is a success. Man, he has a great business!" Parents are helpless: "What can I do? Where we live, we can't keep the kids locked in the apartment. But as soon as they go out in the streets, they get into trouble. I know that my children can get picked up by the police. I can't be with them all the time. I pray to God that someday we can move to the suburbs." The underprivileged are trapped. Both parents have full-time jobs. They come home at night, too tired to talk to their children. The youngsters become part of the street culture. Their values are shaped by the neighborhood gang. The parents do not know what to do. "I used to whip him when he was little, but he grew up. He's too big to spank. So I just let him be. I hope he turns out O.K." Studies have shown that slum children are often subjected to tyrannical parents—or to parents who administer no discipline at all. Homes are often unstable. "Father is never home. Besides, he's not my real father. I think he's the third man my mother has taken up with. He can't tell me what to do. My mother just sits there. She tries to do the right thing. I seldom see my real dad. I don't know what happened to him." Broken homes can mean the collapse of values. A child who is confused and finds no guidance at home will be forced to seek it elsewhere: "We live in a rat-infested hole. My grandmother is raising me. My parents split up last year. I couldn't go with Ma. She has five other younger kids to take care of. So they sent me to live with Grandma. She's a nice old lady. But I don't have much to do with her. I'm on the street a lot. I don't have a room where I can do my homework. Besides, I'm too restless to study. Sure, I smoke pot. In fact, I've tried stronger stuff."

Several years ago I participated in a Religious Youth Weekend Conclave where we gave a questionnaire on drug use to some seventy-three teenagers. Their average age was 16. The questionnaires were unsigned. Seven percent said they had smoked marijuana, none had tried heroin, and 2 percent had taken LSD. They were active members of Temple Youth groups with a high sense of religious commitment. The questionnaires' results were discussed with the group. The majority—middle-class suburban children—were aware of the danger in drug use. The drug users did not say they had used pot. But one could tell from the questions asked in the discussion sessions who had tried marijuana. The pot users tended to be social outcasts and were avoided by the majority of the other youths. I felt that the 7 percent figure of marijuana users was high. Some of the campers may have given false information to confuse us.

So we see that the escape to suburbia is not always the answer. The overprivileged group has its problems, too. Some psychologists hold that middle-class and upper middle-class drug users tend to come from homes with a dominant mother figure and a passive father figure. Children are expected to do well in school. "Everyone goes to college. I better be able to get into a good college." Parents are generous. Children are given material things instead of genuine love. "My mother says she loves me, but she's never home. I can have anything I want, except some of her precious time. I feel like asking her to schedule an appointment to sit down and talk to me. She has time for her clubs and charities. I thought charity begins at home. In our house, Mom only thinks of the 'big issues.' She is busy circulating petitions. I feel like petitioning her to stay home once in a while."

Then, too, as divorce becomes more prevalent and even fashionable, other problems develop: "My folks are divorced. Mom put me in a private school, so she could have more freedom to find a man. She succeeded. I can't stand my stepfather. He's a bore. The headmistress at school caught a gang of us having a pot party in my room. I might get expelled. I'm not worried. My stepfather is loaded. They'll find another school to ship me to if I flunk out here. What a life! Boarding school for nine months, and then two months at summer camp. I have no real home to call my own. My new father resents having me around. Mom acts like a giggling girl around him. She says she loves me

—so long as it is at a distance. I can't wait to grow up and be on my own. In a way, I'm pretty much on my own now."

The middle-class teenager may not be afraid that pot will lead to stronger drugs: "I'll never become a junkie. I can stop smoking grass whenever I want to. I've read up on the subject. Pot is not physically addictive. I don't need pot as a crutch. It's just recreation."

A growing number of teenagers who use pot have no apparent psychological problems. Many appear to be fairly well adjusted in school and at home. They just try pot the way their parents tried cigarettes when they were their age. They like the "high" it gives them. They feel they are safe. They say they will never try any of the hard drugs.

Pot use cuts across all social and cultural lines. From the underprivileged through the middle and upper classes, the pot user is found everywhere—and in apparently increasing numbers. We now speak of the drug culture. At Woodstock in upper New York State, some 300,000 young people gathered. They listened to rock music. Many took drugs. Some became ill. They were well mannered. An adult commented: "I was there. It was frightening. So many young people. All of them so passive. I thought to myself: 'Suppose someone were to take control of them—and lead them like sheep—in some terrible "cause." ' I was really scared." Others praised the exemplary behavior of both youth and police. A patrolman commented: "We couldn't have made drug arrests. There were just too many drug users. The local jails could not hold them. So we did the best we could. We found the young people to be very cooperative. Despite their 'way-out' dress they really were not bad kids. I've changed my mind about the hippies. Things turned out much better than expected."

Penalties for Pot

What keeps youth away from pot? There is the fear that one's future will be adversely affected: "If I get caught with a joint and get a police record, I'll never be able to attend law school. It's a felony to get caught. It isn't worth ruining your life for a cheap thrill." Most states have harsh laws for pot smokers who are apprehended. Disgrace, parental anger, and shame—those are all real possibilities if the law is broken. It is true that public officials have said that the penalties for pot smoking are unreasonably harsh. Yet until the laws are changed, they remain in force. Arrest is a constant fear.

Pot—Harmful?

Is marijuana harmful to your physical health? The hard evidence so far is not conclusive. Tobacco was proven to be harmful after long periods of testing. Pot research to date has shown that it can produce mild euphoria for most users, and some have experienced temporary paranoia. "In some chronic users, even ordinary pot causes personality changes. A high achiever might become apathetic" ("Dangers of Marijuana," by Roland Berg, *Look* magazine, April 15, 1969, p. 46). Emotional dependence is common. "Nor do you need bigger and bigger doses to get your kick. The reverse is true. Old hands get high faster and on smaller amounts than newcomers. Perhaps this indicates a build-up in the brain" (Ibid.). Other effects have been noted by researchers: "Pot smoking will redden your eyes but won't dilate your pupils. It will speed up your pulse but won't alter your breathing. For many persons, it distorts time and changes depth perception; this makes driving a car hazardous" (Ibid.). It may well be that once the scientific evidence is in, marijuana will prove to be the cause of physical and mental damage. So far, it is an open issue. Claims and counterclaims are published. Such was also the case in early tobacco research. The tobacco industry fought the researchers. Even today, the findings on the harmful effects of tobacco are questioned by the tobacco growers and processors. The industry can produce scientists and researchers who claim that tobacco is not injurious to your health. In like manner, as the evidence mounts, we will hear expert opinion that will condemn marijuana and others who will defend its use.

There is another possible result of using pot: "I started on soft drugs. The pusher supplied me with pot. It was cheap. I got a nice little high. After a while, I grew restless. The pusher suggested I try some real stuff. I was introduced to heroin. It cost more. Soon I was hooked. I now work for the pusher. I need "horse" to live. I wish I could stop. You begin with pot and hash. The pusher wants you to 'move up.' He makes a big buck in the hard drugs." Those who start on pot may move up to more potent drugs. So far, only a small precentage of pot users become addicted to the "bigger thrill" drugs. Yet, surveys have also shown that a high percentage of those who become addicts began with marijuana.

Is it worth it to experiment by trying that first joint? The ultimate decision is yours. Are the possible consequences worth the risk? After all the arguments about pot have been stated, we do know that it is illegal. Lawbreaking can be serious, when it's a matter of drugs. It is worth serious thought, before getting involved.

Beyond Pot—LSD

"Diane Linkletter, LSD . . . And Murder." That was the headline in the *Long Island Press,* October 6, 1969. Art Linkletter's daughter leaped to her death under the influence of LSD. "It wasn't suicide," the story quoted him, "because she wasn't herself. It was murder. She was murdered by the people who manufacture and sell LSD."

Diane Linkletter had plunged from a window of her sixth-floor apartment in West Hollywood at 9 A.M. A young man who was with her tried to restrain her. He was too late. What are the facts in the case? Linkletter had known for six months that his daughter was using LSD. She had talked to her father about it. But he was unable to prevent her from continuing to use it. She was

20 years old. She lived in her own apartment. She considered herself an adult. She feared LSD, yet she was unable to avoid it. Linkletter said, "A parent can do little in a case like this. No one can do anything about it, except the young people themselves." Linkletter and his son Jack felt that her death was self-destruction, rather than suicide. Her father wanted other people to know the story. "Otherwise, it's a waste of a wonderful young human life." Diane went with a crowd that experimented with LSD. She found she could not handle it. Her father declared: "It doesn't happen to everyone, but it can happen to anyone." She took LSD some six months prior to her death so as to find relief and escape from problems that troubled her. Instead of relief, she had a very bad "trip," which left her hallucinating long after the effects of the drug should have worn off. The fear of recurrent hallucinations began to work on her. She feared her mind would be destroyed.

The day before her death, she tried LSD again. "She was a loving, happy girl from a family that was always very close and caring," said her father. "She was not in an abyss of melancholy. She was young. Still in her teens, it seemed. And, like all young people, she had problems. Emotional problems. Boy friend problems. Career problems. And always there was the family name to contend with—you know how hard that can be. You're prejudiced by everyone. All of my kids have had to adjust to it, having that name riding on top of them. Diane was very loving and happy—but very emotional. You add LSD to a girl who is somewhat emotional and dramatic, and it can be disastrous. She tried it. The LSD that people shove into their bodies—it's like diving into a pool when you don't have any idea of the depth." Reports indicate that Diane Linkletter was despondent and depressed concerning her identity and her career when the tragedy occurred.

The Linkletter story was but the latest in a series of recent LSD tragedies. As a result, it is felt that young people now tend to avoid LSD. Bad trips do occur. The danger is that once one has taken LSD, "trips" can be repeated without taking more of the drug. "Turn on, tune in, drop out": Dr. Timothy Leary speaks of the liberating religion of LSD. The "trip" becomes the way to a religious experience—if it does not lead to disaster.

Hard Drugs

The "hard-drug scene" is very real. Traffic in strong drugs runs into the millions, if not billions. Fantastic prices are paid for heroin. The drug addict may require $75 daily to sustain his habit. He steals. He will do anything to get the money so as to have his "fix." The world of the addict is nightmarish and unreal. Pot smokers scoff at the danger. "I can stop using grass anytime I wish. I will never try heroin. There is no danger that I will become a junkie. On our campus, pot is in. Junkies are avoided. They are not part of the cool crowd. Junkies are creeps. Who needs them?" College students have little fear of turning to hard drugs.

"Yes, I have friends who smoke pot. One of them went on to heroin. He dropped out of school. I don't know what happened to him. He was a good student. One day he just gave up. I guess he had his problems." College students are not immune to heroin use. Some evidence indicates that hard-drug use is on the increase on the college campus.

The hard-drug scene does indeed exist. It is certainly found in the slum areas of our major cities. Heroin becomes a way of escape from problems. It is the ticket to what the user hopes will be a better world. Instead, he may end up in a nightmarish world of confusion and sickness. Horror stories concerning drug addicts appear daily in the newspapers. Drug raids reveal tremendous caches of hard drugs brought into the country illegally. Pushers roam the streets. Money changes hands. Customers are plentiful. Young girls sell their bodies to sustain their habit. The police do what they can. Enough has been written about the junkie to fill an entire library. The addict considers himself a failure. He has little regard for his own worth. He feels he can never succeed in life. Anything he has tried to do has led to failure. He drifts along. He has no goals. He has little sense of value. He has few, if any, close friends. Those who love him now avoid him. He is alone, except for others who share his habit. Even here, friendships are transient. Junkies use each other to sustain their habit. They may share a "bag." Yet they tend to be very private persons. They are loners.

Contrary to popular belief, hard drugs do not stimulate one's sexual desires. Instead, they tend to make you lethargic. Girls who become prostitutes to get money for heroin are deriving no pleasure from their profession. The junkie lives for the moment of relief that the needle brings. He has no control over his life. He roams the streets like an animal. The need for a fix drives him to a life of crime. He does not steal for the enjoyment and the thrill of it. He steals only to get money to buy the drug that can give him temporary relief. He may well be filled with self-hate. Unless he finds his way to a drug treatment center for help, he can die alone, untended and unloved. What is happening in the world is of little concern to him. He has no interests, other than getting the "stuff." He will do literally anything to get enough stuff to sustain his habit. He is like a rat trapped in a maze, with no way out. This is the junkie. He is a leper to society. He is shunned. Those wishing to open drug treatment centers find it hard to rent property. "We don't want junkies in our neighborhood. Take your treatment center elsewhere. We don't want our kids to see those people. Besides, they are criminals. They will ruin the neighborhood." The junkie engenders fear. Society is frightened.

Who should be jailed—the junkie and the pusher, or just the pusher? The debate goes on. Some call for legalizing drug use: "If it is available at legal centers—and is cheap enough—then the junkie won't have to rob and kill for money to get his fix." Others reply: "If you make it legal, more will try it. In the open, it just encourages drug use and abuse."

Society is unsure how to combat addiction. Methadone has been tried. It is a drug itself, used to wean heroin addicts from their habit. In places such as Topic House and Synanon, ex-addicts work with patients to try to bring them back to a normal life. Professionals in the field of medicine are using ex-addicts more and more in combating the menace of drug addiction: "I am an ex-addict. I talk their language. I've been there—and I came back. They can relate to me. They cannot relate to a doctor who has never been on drugs. We share a common experience. I was once part of their world. I could go back to that world to-morrow, if I took one shot of heroin." Treatment centers meet with varying degrees of success. More youths become addicted each year. The problem has not been solved.

Heroin is showing up more and more on high school and even junior high school campuses. New Yorkers were shocked by the testimony of a 12 year old "pusher" who started on heroin at the age of 10. Statistics reveal a dramatic increase in deaths from heroin in the under 20 age category. A slum-dweller remarks: "Now that heroin use is increasing in middle-class neighborhoods, maybe we'll get some action to eliminate it."

Drugs and the New Morality

How is drug use related to the new morality? A parent says: "There is something immoral about drug use. It is immoral to walk away from life and its problems. A moral person is a person who assumes responsibility." Religion teaches that man must be active in the world. The Hebrew Prophet Micah declared, "For what does the Lord require of Thee, but to do justly, love mercy, and walk humbly with Thy God." Religion gives you values. Religion can provide the setting for making a moral commitment. The youth who is busy with constructive tasks has less time for drugs. One youth declares, "Who needs drugs? I've got plenty to do. I'm active in school in the Debating Club. I am on the executive board of my Temple Youth Group. I work hard in local politics. I have plenty of homework. When I get a chance, I play some baseball with my friends. Why fool around with something that can only get you into trouble?"

The moral tone of our society calls for young people to be

busy and active with school work, sports, hobbies, and other outside interests. Pot is associated—in adult eyes—with long, dirty
hair, strange dress, funny glasses, a glazed look, and a chalky
white face. Adults believe that no pot smoker would be clean-
cut, beardless, and Ivy League in appearance. Adults may well
be fooled. Recent evidence suggests that the "Ivy League," clean-
cut businessman type may also use drugs from time to time.
Possibly such a person would not use hard drugs. Soft drugs
would be something else. One hears talk of the pot-smoking
young junior executive.

Few people believe that drug use can be limited by a harsh
law-and-order crackdown on pot smokers. Heroin and related
drugs are something else again. Many feel that the hard-drug
pushers should be dealt with severely, and the manufacturers of
hard products be given long jail sentences. At the other end of
the spectrum are those who hold that turning users and pushers
into criminals is the wrong way. Many say, "Let's make pot
legal." Or: "Let's take another look at how we treat heroin
addicts. Let's give them what they need to keep going and out of
jail." In New York State, a plan was tried to force addicts to
go to rehabilitation centers. The plan has met with mixed results.

There does not seem to be just one way suddenly to solve
the drug problem. A variety of approaches is in effect. All have
had some degree of success. The addict has little self-pride. He
has self-hate. He feels he is worthless. He drives himself forward,
almost as if he had a death wish. He is a sick person. How shall
we treat his sickness? Is jail the answer? How can he be cured
and returned to society? What safeguards can be employed to
prevent him from going back on drugs? An addict says, "I've
been 'cured' dozens of times. When I feel I am really in bad
shape, I turn myself in to a hospital. They get me back to fairly
good shape. I go back on the streets. I want to start a new life.
But how can I? So I drift back to the only friends I have. Soon
I'm on the stuff. It's a vicious cycle. I don't know how to break
out of it."

Society knows the goals. The addict must be cured, rehabilitated, given a decent job, psychiatric help to rebuild his self-image, and placed in a situation in which he can make the right kind of friends. But how can these goals be attained? Where shall society find the money to do the job? The Youth Group of the congregation I serve has a project. It raises money for Topic House, a drug treatment center on Long Island. Topic House works with youths who are trying to stay off drugs. Topic House residents and their doctors have spoken to our congregation on the Sabbath. The young people have listened. The project to support Topic House was very successful. Young people do have a feeling of compassion for other youngsters. As a teenager, you might wish to get involved in a project to offer help to an addict center. There might be some parental resistance. But most of the centers have tours during which the community is invited to see their facilities. Once a parent visits the center, he is not likely to oppose helping such a place.

The addict who knows that society cares can be rehabilitated. He can rebuild the image of himself. If he is wanted and loved he can be restored to a decent life. It is certainly a moral act to help one's neighbor who is in distress. All religions approve of this. "Love thy neighbor as thyself." Love can mean getting involved with those who are sick. Addicts are sick. They are sick in the sense that they feel that they are nothing. When convinced they are something and can become somebody, a miraculous change can occur. A Topic House patient, age 23, spoke at our Temple. He was asked how he got on drugs. "I was not accepted by the intellectuals at our school. I didn't have any friends. I really tried to get in with the right crowd. The intellectuals wanted no part of me. My grades in school were poor. I was told that I was not college material. I wanted friends. I got in with a crowd that used pot. From pot, we went on to other things. I needed money. I finally stole a car. I was arrested. Now I'm on my way back to a normal life. I am learning from the doctors at Topic House that I have to have respect for myself as a person."

To help others rebuild their lives is certainly a highly moral act. The heroes of all religions were men who worked with the lowly and the needy. Poverty does not mean only physical hunger. It can also involve those who are starved by lack of self-respect. Many persons hunger for at least some degree of success. Without values and goals, life becomes intolerable. The drug addict may believe he is beyond hope. To restore his will to live is certainly a moral matter.

A Casual Concern?

Can we be casual about drug use? It would seem that we cannot be indifferent. Crime is on the increase. Much of it is committed by the drug addict. Arrests are made. Rehabilitation is more difficult. The cycle of drug use, stealing, arrest, and then stealing—and more arrests—such a cycle is real. A moral society cannot be casual in the face of what is going on.

What Can You Do?

Before experimenting with pot, I would suggest you do the following: Discuss drugs with your parents. They may be more helpful than you think. Talk to friends and others your age who have different points of view on drug use. Don't just talk to those who favor trying pot. Seek out those who have not started. Find out why they have avoided grass and hash. Look into the laws of your community. Is it worth having your name on a police record for one moment of excitement?

Most heroin addicts began with pot. The first step to heroin is the use of grass. Are you strong enough to stop at the marijuana level of drug use? Many do go on to the hard drugs. Over 90 percent of the heroin users started with pot.

Ask yourself, "Why do I want to try a joint?" Is it because you just want to try something new? Not everything offered should be taken. Are all your friends joining the drug scene? You can find other friends who are not part of the drug crowd.

If you are convinced that drugs are harmful, then you can

talk to your friends who are on drugs—and try to persuade them to stop, or to seek help if they are far into the drug scene.

If you are active in a civic or religious club or group, you may want to look into the drug situation in your community. You may find that there are drug treatment centers that need financial aid. You may wish to raise money for their needs.

When your school has films and speakers on drug abuse, go to those programs with an open mind. "Scare" films have little value. But even the worst of them present elements of truth. Keep an open mind. All the evidence on marijuana is not in as yet. Why start with something that may prove to be unhealthful? As of the moment, pot is illegal. It is likely to remain so.

The decision, finally, will be your own to make. Read up on the arguments. Discuss them with your family and friends. Think before you act!

CHAPTER VII

What Makes a Moral Person?

I asked the parent of two teenage sons, "What do you think your children would say about the morality of the world today?"

She answered quickly, "Rabbi, the younger generation cannot stand our hypocrisy. We say one thing and do something else. Our youth are not rejecting the Ten Commandments, the Bill of Rights, or the Constitution. What they are rejecting is the fact that we pay lip service to these values but do not live by them. We say we believe in peace, but there is war. We declare that poverty is bad, yet slums exist. They share the same values as we have—though perhaps they are slightly more liberal on the matter of sex or drugs—but they deeply resent our doing so little to alleviate the situations prevalent around them."

Many of you would agree with this discerning parent. Morality means to practice what you preach. A moral person does not say one thing and then do something else. A moral person does not just give lip service to a cause. Morality means to live a certain way. You seem to be saying that it is almost better not to enunciate high ideals (then not follow them) than to say them in the first place. Perhaps silence is best, unless one intends to act in a moral manner. The church and synagogue are not criticized because of their ideals. In fact, much of the idealism of youth grows out of the teachings of the world's religions. Youth searches through Christianity, Judaism, and the Eastern faiths for a basis for belief and understanding. Your generation enjoys discussion, to be sure. But discussion that leads nowhere is rejected.

You are more willing than your parents to take risks. "My son wanted to attend the peace moratorium march in Washington. I would not let him go. I was afraid that there would be violence. He stayed home. He resented my attitude." Such words are spoken by parents. They are concerned about you. They have raised you, and watched you grow and develop. They may limit your freedom to act because they fear for your welfare. The young are impatient. You plan, and dream, and do. Parents agree with your ideas, but may also limit your ability to carry them out. Conflict arises between the generations when parents give lip service to the same goals as the youth's—then are fearful to let the young person act out his passionate feelings.

The mood of the parent differs from that of the youth. Parents have experienced more and lived longer. They have seen much. They may feel that events tend to repeat themselves. One parent declared, "I was born at the wrong time. When I was a child, we obeyed our parents. I looked forward to the time when I would become an adult, and then be able to exert some authority. I grew up, and now my children dominate me. I have never had a chance to exercise control. Today, there is no respect for authority."

Today, respect must be earned. It is not automatically conferred. Young people need to be convinced that any adult figure is correct. An open society demands open answers. A public figure takes a position on a national issue. His son may march in a demonstration that opposes his father's beliefs. The fact that a father permits his son to oppose him would be an approved moral act. It would be immoral for a father to deny his son the right to act, merely for appearances' sake. A teenager says, "Why are you so worried about what others will say or think? Why can't you act according to what you believe? Why do you make me dress in a certain way? Is it because you believe that is how I should dress, or are you more concerned over what the neighbors might say?" Morality might be termed how one defines right or wrong. A moral person is true to his convictions—no matter what personal sacrifice is involved. He acts as he speaks. He speaks as he acts. He is not disjointed. He is joined to the world through thought, speech, and deed.

Morality is very much a "now" matter. It involves what is happening today—at this very moment. A man lands on the moon. Why does a slum exist at the very moment of that achievement in outer space? Some young people find it immoral and intolerable that science gives us excitement and progress while men die on far-off battlefields. An older morality would say that war is inevitable. Someone will always be fighting and dying, somewhere in the world. There will always be starving people somewhere on the globe. You do not accept the inevitability of suffering. A comedian commented, "When I was a child, my mother told me to finish the food on my plate because people were starving in Europe. I ate everything and got fat. But it didn't help the starving people. They were still hungry." The parent says you should be so grateful for the blessings of good food that it would be sinful not to eat everything served to you. Youth cannot accept such a concept. If others are hungry, then we should sacrifice what we have so as to feed them. You tend to take sharing seriously. The swollen bellies of Biafran children horrified you. Adults were also bothered by the Biafran babies. Your sense of horror seems to go deeper than that of the adult world. Youth responds quickly to pleas for help. Your spirit of altruism is genuine. You care.

Concerned young persons are less given to equivocation than are adults. You see a problem, and if it is a moral issue you have the energy and determination to do something positive. You are impatient with bureaucracy. If a problem exists, solve it now. You have a great sense of urgency. To delay is immoral. Your sense of priorities is such that moral matters are at the top of the agenda. I am convinced that you care deeply. You do pass moral judgments on both people and events. You push ahead if you are convinced that the cause is right. Your concern for others is positive. "My children do not disagree with our values. They are only horrified that we say one thing and do something else."

You *are* morality. Each of us is a walking, talking, acting example of morality or immorality. Morality involves the total person. Your sense of values make you what you are—and what you hope to become. You pass quick judgment on those who do not measure up to your moral code. You do not grant your peers or adults the right to be immoral. If you are sad, it is because so much injustice exists in the world. Men shuffle papers while other men fight, die, and starve. To be unmoved is immoral. Not to care is the sin of the moment. To know that starvation exists and not to act—that is the height of hypocrisy.

Roadblocks to Morality

Critics of America have called us a completely secularized society that worships the dollar. We have been labeled the affluent society that cares only about the consumption of goods and services. The American ideal is pictured in the minds of Europeans as the man with the bulging wallet who cares only for his own personal enjoyment. To be American is to be rich, successful, and unconcerned. Despite the billions of dollars America has given away in foreign aid, and despite the old war debts still owed to us, we still come in for a great deal of criticism.

We tend to be our own most severe critics. The guitar-playing protest folk singers tell of an America that is ruled by militarism and grinds the poor Vietnamese under foot while the war profiteers of the industrial-military complex enrich themselves. America is called the land of ABM and the hydrogen bomb. We are labeled an expansionist power, seeking to conquer Southeast Asia. Many of those who have severely condemned our Asian policy were silent when Russian tanks occupied Czechoslovakia. Those same groups said little when the rulers of China conducted massive purges using Red Guard students to bring the intellectuals into line. The radical left has castigated Israel for her attitude toward Arab refugees while failing to mention that Arab states still practice the enslavement of Negroes in the Sudan.

Within our own borders, the crisis involving black and white relationships is far from resolved. White middle-class teachers

in the slums of Harlem are resented by black parents. The black
P.T.A. and militant groups cry aloud for black principals and
teachers. They argue that a black child cannot identify with a
white middle-class teacher. The fight to gain local control by
local school boards in New York is an example of the cancerous
sore of virulent racism. In some school districts busing and the
pairing of grades is practiced. Under the pairing approach, all
the children who are in a given grade go to the same school, thus
forcing integration. The plan has met with some success. Busing
to effect integration has been criticized. Arguments are made.
"A child who is bused does not have time to make friends with
the other children in the school. He cannot stay for after-school
activities. He cannot develop a loyalty to that school. No child
should be bused out of his neighborhood." The argument is often
put on a moral basis: "It is immoral to force integration." Or,
"It is immoral not to force integration." "We have to wait for
people to be ready to integrate." "The law cannot change human
nature. To go slow is best."

Militants of the radical left and the radical right do seem to
be in harmony at times: "Since people are not ready for integration, and never will be—then let us create all-black schools and
thereby build black pride. Only blacks can really teach blacks.
Only blacks can understand the black problems." A cry goes out
for racial quotas in the colleges. Some black leaders push hard
for a minimum number of blacks to be admitted to a college,
whether or not the students have the academic qualifications.
Intensive summer courses are offered to prepare black students
for college entrance. Black-studies programs become a part of
college, as well as of high-school curricula—when the demands
are made.

Is there a moral obligation to work for an integrated society?
Will integration destroy the black heritage and pride in "black-
ness" that some black leaders seek desperately to attain? How
moral is it to call the Negro who works for an integrated society
an Uncle Tom? Those are some of the complex issues that affect
us. You want to be a moral person. You care about your fellow

man. What shall you do? Are there some areas of agreement for all teenagers, whatever their race or religion?

The Agony of Vietnam

While driving home, I listened, on my car radio, to a "talk" show. It centered on the slaying of innocent civilians in My Lai hamlet in Vietnam. One panelist felt that the accused soldiers were being tried on television and in the press, before a military court could be convened to determine innocence or guilt. Another panelist argued just as forcefully that if the press and TV had not brought the facts before the public, the Army would never have fully investigated the alleged massacre.

Defenders of the My Lai incident declared that in war men do terrible things under the pressure of battle. "My buddy had been killed by the V.C. When I went into that village, I only wanted to kill the V.C. in revenge." A heartbroken father declares, "If I had been in that company, I would have shot the commanding officer who made a butcher out of my son."

Where is the moral issue? Is it more moral to drop a bomb from a plane that kills civilians than to shoot a 2-year-old baby at close range? One ex-GI who had been at My Lai said, "When I saw them shooting children, I felt they really went too far." The image of the friendly GI Joe of World War II has been tarnished. How much guilt and how deep a guilt feeling can a nation endure? The Germans have become weary of our reminders of their atrocities under Hitler. Can Americans stand the constant attack on our moral posture in wartime?

Americans have never feared introspection. We are, if anything, overly critical of ourselves. That is part of our strength. We believe in fair play. We try to live by the rules of the game. Even if the other side massacres the innocent, we like to believe that we are above such conduct. Right will win out in the end. The guilty must be punished. The military may indicate that a soldier should not obey an illegal order. But on the battlefield, who is to challenge one's superior officer? The soldier fights as he is directed. It is alleged that in My Lai the men were just doing their job. But Sgt. Michael Bernhard, who was there, declared, "It was point-blank murder." He claims he told officers, "The hell with this. I'm not doing it."

It would seem to me that Sgt. Bernhard expressed a higher morality in his refusal to kill civilians. Others would argue that a good soldier follows orders.

Is it immoral to make money from selling pictures of a massacre to the newspapers and magazines? A former Army photographer sold his My Lai atrocity pictures to *Life* magazine—for a sum in five figures. Another ex-GI who was also at My Lai said, "I won't talk to another reporter unless I get paid." Many were sickened by the entire incident. The accusation was made that the My Lai incident was hushed up until after the November 1969 Peace Moratorium march, for fear the telling of it might arouse the marchers to violence.

Morality involves doing the right thing. In wartime, our national government sets certain standards of conduct to be implemented on the battlefield. Someone asked, "Are those of us who sit at home any less guilty for the My Lai affair than the soldiers whom we drafted and sent to the jungles of Vietnam?"

Technology does not make it easier to be moral. It can make it more difficult. A bomber pilot does not see his victims. A man on the ground does see those he kills. The Bible says, "Thou shalt not kill." Young people wonder if killing is ever really justified.

Nazi Germany employed genocide as an instrument of national policy. Innocent civilians—most of them Jewish—were systematically put to death in the concentration camps. It is not American policy to kill innocent civilians in Vietnam. There is a difference in the degree of immorality between Auschwitz and Songmy. Neither is morally defensible. The American action at My Lai, however, evoked strong protest from military and civilian authorities. The alleged perpetrators of the massacre were brought to trial in an American military court. On the other hand, Germans slaughtered civilians as part of a deliberate policy to exterminate what they termed the "Jewish race."

Morality Equals Honesty

"I don't care what a person does, so long as he is honest about it." That is one of those broad statements that bear examination. The old definition of honesty involved doing the right thing. "When I was growing up, my parents would whip me if they caught me stealing. I was in mortal fear of the woodshed. Today, the kids aren't afraid of anything or anybody. We knew it was dishonest to steal. We had respect for the policeman on the beat. Kids today have no morals. They are dishonest with their parents—and even with their friends." That is the charge leveled at the younger generation.

Youth has responded that honesty is more than obeying the law. Honesty becomes an attitude. It involves saying what you really think, and doing what you really believe is right. That can mean breaking an unjust law. It can involve joining protesters in a work stoppage at a construction site. It can mean joining a sit-in of grape-pickers at a migrant village. Honesty becomes a form of action.

If the law can be broken because I think it is unjust, then we see a shift in the moral pattern. Moral standards for the group become more difficult to set. If each individual must do his own thing because he knows it is best, then who is to say that the K.K.K. cannot do its own thing, even as S.D.S. seeks to do its own thing? That is the argument against honesty's equaling morality. If I honestly feel that the only way to improve the city is to burn down the house of an incompetent mayor, shall I do it? A few have chosen self-immolation to dramatize a point: the burning monks of Vietnam were an embarrassment to our government. Those monks were doing their own thing to protest repression through unjust laws.

Does the murder of one's opponent become the ultimate act

of honesty? During World War II, if an assassin had been able to kill Hitler, he would have been hailed as a hero. Is assassination ever justified? Do we kill tyrants? What is an honest act, and what is dishonest? Victims of the Nazis were saved when charitable persons hid them in defiance of the Nazi laws. The Nuremberg court held Nazi racial laws to be unjust.

"Any act is moral, so long as it does not harm my fellow man. Any act that unfairly restricts him is dishonest—and must be opposed." Would you agree with that statement?

Civil Dissent

"Willingness to incur the wrath and punishment of government," said Mrs. Patricia Robert Harris, professor of law at Howard University and former Ambassador to Luxembourg, "can represent the highest loyalty and respect for a democratic society. Such respect and self-sacrifice may well prevent, rather than cause violence" (*New York Times,* Dec. 9, 1969, page 1). Mrs. Harris made her declaration as the National Commission on the Causes and Prevention of Violence was about to make its final report. She was part of the minority that opposed the final wording of the report. She stood with those, including Milton Eisenhower, who held that acceptance of penalty is sometimes the only way of changing the law. "If the majority's doctrine of 'everyone wait until the outcome of the one individual test case' had been applied by black Americans in the nineteen-sixties, probably not one present major civil rights statute would have been enacted," said Judge Higginbotham, another commission member who voted with the minority (Ibid., page 44). He was supported by Senator Philip Hart of Michigan who declared, "I feel that history will continue to note circumstances when it is not immoral to be illegal" (Ibid., page 44).

The majority opinion of the commission denied that they had any racial bias: "Every time a court order is disobeyed, each time an injunction is violated, each occasion on which a court decision is flouted, the effectiveness of our judicial system is eroded. How much erosion can be tolerated?" (Ibid., page 44). They saw a danger that continuing massive disobedience—even of a nonviolent nature—could lead to anarchy in the nation. If individuals or groups continue to decide for themselves which laws are objectionable, "we shall face nationwide disobedience of many laws and thus anarchy" (Ibid., page 1).

The split in the thinking of the commission reflects the division of thought among Americans. The majority report held that "massive civil disobedience, even the nonviolent kind inspired by Gandhi and the Rev. Dr. Martin Luther King, Jr., could lead to anarchy in the United States." The minority disagreed, and did not feel that all dissenters should abide by the law until it was tested in the courts. They could envision situations in which unjust laws—still pending court action—should be opposed. So long as an individual was willing to accept legal penalty for opposing a law considered unjust, there was no real threat to our government.

Here we have a moral issue. Should you respond to a higher law if you are convinced that a civil regulation is oppressive and unjust? Sit-ins in segregated lunch counters broke down local laws and customs. Protests against segregated schools led to changes in the law, and a landmark Supreme Court decision. Activists will argue that unless unjust laws are fought, they will never be repealed. Nonactivists respond that gradual change may mean justice delayed, but when justice is finally attained, it will have wider popular support. At what point does legitimate dissent become criminal anarchy? Is it moral to storm the Pentagon or the Justice Department in defiance of the law? Is burning a draft card an act of civil or criminal dissent?

The moral issue remains. The Violence Commission's majority report reflects the growing concern of many Americans that continuing acts of civil disobedience may undermine our government. Others have responded that the fear is not justified, and they believe that failure to actively oppose unfair laws is immoral.

The Honest Person

Who is the honest person? Is it the person who always speaks his mind? There are times to keep silent, so as not to hurt others. Your friend wears an unattractive dress. Should you tell her what you think of her outfit? If she asks your opinion, then you can tell her in a tactful way what you think. If she does not ask your opinion, then silence may be best.

A story is told of a very ugly girl and a very ugly boy who fell in love. They were both lonely. They had few friends. After their marriage, they went to live in a small cottage in the woods. Soon, a miracle occurred. Through the eyes of love, each appeared to be beautiful to the other. They thought their home possessed some rare magic. Now that they were no longer ugly they invited their friends to a party so that their friends could see how they had changed. The friends came. The couple looked the same to them. But in the radiance of love, the ugly pair saw only beauty in each other. The magic was in them—and not in the house where they dwelt. The opinion of their friends was unimportant.

A bank robber confesses that he has committed a crime. He gives an honest account of his deed. That does not make him a moral person. A rapist is caught in the act of molesting a young girl. He confesses to his crime. It is an honest confession to the attempt to perform an immoral act. Morality and honesty are not the same. It is wrong to say, "The truly moral person is honest. He tells it like it is, even if it hurts." A Nazi could honestly believe that Hitler was right. That did not make him a moral person. "I am innocent. I only did what I was told. I acted under orders. I am an honest man." In a sense, such a person is honest. He tells the truth as he understands it. His actions are not moral. The new morality comes down hard on the side of justice for the oppressed. The honest act is the act of compassion. It stems from a concern with the welfare of others.

Do our actions flow from what we really want? Where do we get our ideas as to what is right or wrong? Is any man a complete individualist? No man stands alone. What I think is best is not always a private concern. As a member of the human race, I am part of the herd, whether I wish to be or not. I may make a decision, and I may implement it. But the decision involves society. Society is not isolated persons. It concerns community and communities.

Challenge to Parents

Convince, do not legislate. Set an example. Let your actions speak louder than your words. Are these mere clichés, or are they the building-blocks of a relationship?

The older morality was the blueprint of another age. It could deal in absolutes. You were expected to do what age and experience considered to be correct. Tradition was handed down from father to son. Each generation had obligations inherited from a previous age. Religion stressed this idea. A young man tells his father that he is in love with a girl of another faith. The father says, "Do you have the right to betray the heritage you received from Abraham, Isaac, and Jacob? Do you not owe your religion something?" The youth is unmoved. He is in love. His commitment is to the here and now. The new morality looks upon the past as useful, but not binding. Unless it can make sense, it does not influence action. Religion, to be "with it," must reflect current concerns. The past is interesting, romantic, and nice. It bears small relationship to present decisions. What does religion say today? What is wrong with intermarriage if two people love each other? Love, and not religious belief, becomes the standard. To please the older generation, a couple may seek out a clergyman who will perform an intermarriage. The verb "convert" becomes distasteful: "I didn't even ask her what her religion was until after we became engaged. Religion is not that important to either one of us."

Absolutes begin to crumble. Even dress codes for worship services have been modified. To say the words, "religious services" to a member of the older generation brings forth the image of well-dressed persons sitting quietly in the pews of a temple or a church. The same words—even for religious youth, may conjure up the picture of a group of boys and girls sitting around a campfire singing protest songs, interspersed with spontaneous prayers. "I can really pray at youth camp. The stars are the roof above. My comrades in prayer are my friends. I sit on the ground, and not in an upholstered pew. Somehow, the outdoor service brings me closer to God." Campfire religion has been criticized by some clergymen: "Where are the youth on Friday night or Sunday morning? Why do they enjoy services so much at camp, and at home they stay away?" We discussed the folk-rock ritual as one answer. We spoke of the coffee-house services. The absolutes have disappeared.

In the new "radical" age, your advice is being sought. Parents have begun to turn to youth for some answers. If the absolutes are to be set aside, how shall authority function?

What Is Left to Believe In?

Absolutes have been eroded. Spokesmen for religion are seldom consulted, unless they have established themselves as revivalists or TV personalities. The clergy cast about—almost in desperation—for a way to the hearts of the young people. The youth priest or youth rabbi is engaged to stir up interest among the young people. Religionists recognize that trouble is brewing. Does the synagogue have a future? Will the churches of the next generation be empty? Those are real questions. Religionists seek some new approaches to old problems. Even radical solutions are considered. James Forman's demand for "Black reparations" has stirred a response in a few church circles. The religions of America seek to be relevant. The question is—how?

Instead of using the word "commanded" or "you must," religionists use terms such as "value." What are your values in life? Is immediate gratification the goal of the human experience? Are we to be mere collectors of moments of pleasure? Shall life be one long search for the next thrill? Or is there a deeper pleasure in joys delayed? Will we enjoy a car more if we wait until we can earn the money ourselves to purchase it?

Parents have learned that they cannot buy your love. Gifts are no substitute for care and concern—and being there when you need them. Some youths have reacted against luxury. Some have lost faith in a society built on consumption and acquisition of things. They will say that technology produces the "plastic" man—who is strong, but can be easily broken. They do not wish to turn into the 9-to-5 robot, who has a small niche in a large corporation. They are searching for values. More and more you hear, "What do I really want out of life? I'm not sure. Whatever it is, it isn't what my dad is doing. I know he hates his job. I often wonder why he sticks it out, when he could be happier doing something else. He wanted to become an artist. Now he works in an agency doing advertising layouts. He is bored. He doesn't get a kick out of life. He just goes through the motions. His life is not satisfying."

Young people fear the trap of adulthood. You do not want to make a mistake. You see the fears, frustrations, and anxieties that haunt many of your parents. "How can I, at age 18, make a decision as to my career—when I may have to live with that decision when I am 45?" Your parent, who is middle-aged, may wonder, "How unfair of the world to have demanded that I decide, at age 20, what I'm stuck with doing now. I have obligations. I have children to raise—a wife to care for. Where can I go at my age? What company will hire a man who is past 40? I'd better play it safe, and hold on to what I've got."

The older we get, the less inclined we are to take chances. Sometimes a father hesitates to change jobs. He does not wish to uproot his children in the middle of their high-school years. He is far from sure that to engage in a new venture will be any better than what he is doing now. The older generation longs for a measure of security: "I have almost twenty years in with the company. I will get a nice pension when I retire, if I can stick it out for another fifteen years. It's too late for me to look for another career."

"I dream of the time when I retire. I look forward to a small home in the country. The children will be grown up and married. Then I will really enjoy life."

Some do live on the dreams of joy delayed. The American ethic calls for hard work now and relaxation later. At least an earlier ethic said that. Times are changing. Can we still believe in the work ethic? Some youths would like to drift. The movie *Easy Rider* shows us this side of youth's desire to drift from adventure to adventure.

In a world without standards it is difficult to be an effective parent. Adults are more fixed in their patterns of thought and action. The longer you live, the more likely are your ideas to crystallize.

Old Values—Gone?

What has happened to the old values of love of flag and country—and cleanliness? Long hair and dirt and disrespect for the government have replaced the earlier virtues. "I'm too proud to ask for welfare. Inflation eats up everything. We may have to sell our home. My salary has not kept pace with living costs. I have to sweat and work hard, while those others sit around and collect welfare checks. And they can cause rioting and looting—and no one cares. Even the police stand around."

"Membership in my union is a private matter. I should have the same right to hand my work tools to my son, even as the owner of the corner grocery store has the right to turn over his business to his son. Keep them out of our union." Such sentiments are expressed more often than one would care to admit. There is a reaction to change. America is far from a radical society. A strong feeling of conservatism runs through the American system.

Change comes slowly. Ethnic minorities have discovered that riots and demands can accomplish only so much. Polls show that white middle-class America doesn't want the Negro to move too fast. Even more ominous, some polls would indicate that a sizable group are fearful that the blacks have gained too much already. "To succeed in America, it is better to be black. You can get a job, even if you are incompetent. You can be on welfare, and drive a new car. Even the police will treat a black man with more respect than he will a white man. I cannot turn on the TV without seeing a black face." Such remarks are not uncommon. They represent the fear of change.

The "Now" Generation

The word "now" sums up the desires of youth. Your generation wants many things at once. Your parents had the same desires. But they could not attain them as easily. You want an immediate end to war, poverty, slums, the draft, abortion laws, and drug raids. Young people are impatient. They have always longed to take over. The young have always secretly (or openly) felt they could do better than their parents. Those who fought in World War II blamed their parents for the isolationism that produced a Hitler. Those who fought in Vietnam blame the over-30 generation for involving us in a costly land war in Asia. When you reach adulthood, your children will find fault with you for whatever is troubling the world—be it slums, air pollution, overpopulation, or whatever.

To live means to exist with a certain amount of tension. To live means to have problems. Your generation wishes to see some hope of the resolving of major crises. You cannot easily understand a society at war in Asia—and, periodically, seemingly at war with itself. You not only want solutions "now," but you want idealism to permeate mankind. Your vision is of a world of love and peace. It is a society in which all men are brothers and can live in such a way that they smile at one another—and do not hurt one another. It is a utopian vision in which, for example, prisons will either be abolished or used as humane retraining centers for those hostile to society. Your vision

includes a world in which each man will have enough to eat—
and have employment that will give dignity and purpose to his
days on earth.

The Youthful Activist

Not all are passive flower children. Your generation has produced an impressive number of activists: "We want change *now*.
We want an end to war *now*. We want an end to the draft *now*.
We want racial justice *now*." The insistent and incessant chant
calls for change *now*. It is having an effect.

On October 15, 1969, young people participated in Vietnam
Moratorium Day. Throughout the nation rallies were held. Thousands gathered to listen to speeches by political leaders. Prayer
vigils for peace were held in synagogues and churches. Both
young and old wore peace buttons. Almost no violence occurred,
although two teenagers did commit suicide to protest the war.
For the most part, Moratorium Day activities were carried out
with quiet dignity. The morning of October 15, I stood in front
of the Levittown library where several hundred young people
had assembled for a peace march. They were led by a young
teacher. He told the crowd, "Many of you may be new to marches.
This is nonviolent protest. People may yell at you and taunt you.
Don't yell back. Hold to your line of march. No matter how you
are provoked, do not answer. Keep marching." Silently they
filed out for a five-mile march to Hofstra University. It was more
than just a day off from school. Those young people truly believed that the war could end only if they did something about it.
That same night, I helped to lead prayers for peace at our temple. The service was composed by the youth. Adults also presented
readings. Songs were sung. A guitar was played. Later many
joined a candlelight peace vigil parade to Eisenhower Park.

Democracy, with all its imperfections, does give wide latitude
for dissent.

The day after Moratorium Day, the Mets won the World
Series. New Yorkers went wild. An impromptu ticker-tape bar-

rage was unleashed from the New York skyscrapers. People wanted something to cheer about. The previous day, some drove with lights on to show disapproval of the peace activities. Others displayed the American flag to show what they considered to be patriotism in the face of the demonstrators. Yet only a day later, peace marchers and government supporters could cheer together for the home team as it won victory. The violinist Isaac Stern commented: "If the Mets can win the Series, then even peace is possible."

We live in the age of miracles. Youth itself is a time of strength. Young people will try almost anything. Your generation never says "no." The impossible swiftly becomes the possible, if you care, and if you act. All will agree that war is immoral. It is sometimes employed to defend one's country. Various paths to peace have been proposed. You can do your part, as you study the issues. The decision is yours. Your thoughts have an effect. Moratorium Day began with the youth. The idea then quickly spread to the older generation. Mayor John Lindsay of New York ordered flags on public buildings flown at half-staff. A late session of Congress was held to debate the war. Many "doves" in Congress suddenly emerged. Youth was the catalyst. In mid-November 1969, a quarter of a million people assembled at the Washington Monument to participate in the New Mobilization. Youth *can* motivate and innovate. Youth power is real. When it is harnessed to morality, it can be a powerful force for good.

How shall we understand the generation gap? A story from Jewish tradition is helpful: "When Rabbi Noah, the son of Rabbi Lekhovitz, assumed the succession after his father's death, his disciples noticed that there were a number of ways in which he did not conduct himself as his father had, and asked him about this. 'I do just as my father did,' he replied. 'He did not imitate, and I do not imitate'" (Borowitz, Eugene B., *A New Jewish Theology in the Making*, page 146. The Westminster Press, Philadelphia, 1968).

CHAPTER VIII

Where Do We Go from Here?

An old man was seen planting a tree. A young man mocked him. "Why do you waste your time? You will never live long enough to enjoy its fruits."

The elder replied, "I am not doing this for myself. This is for the next generation. Someone planted trees so that I could enjoy their fruit and shade. I shall do the same for those who shall follow after me."

Like the elderly gentleman in the story, we work not just for today. What we do has its effect on those who will follow us. In making moral decisions we must think of the future. In devising a code for morality it is wise to consider what is yet to be. "I see nothing wrong in premarital intercourse." A young man made that statement. I said to him, "How would you feel if you were a parent and it was your daughter who was to engage in such an act?" The teenager paused and reflected, "You know, I never thought of that."

Think Before You Act

What you do does have an effect on others. The boy who uses a girl for his own pleasure, then boasts to others of his exploits, is possibly destroying the young woman who shared her favors with him. The youth who- stands by while he hears a friend being slandered and gossiped about—such a person may be acting in an immoral way. "Do not stand idly by" might well be a moral consideration.

A young woman is savagely attacked. She screams. No one comes to her aid. No one wishes to get involved. A mentally sick

146

patient climbs out onto the roof of a hospital. He wavers unde-
cidedly. The crowd below begins to chant, "Chicken, chicken,
jump, jump." A doctor brings the man's family to him, and he
rushes away from the ledge. The crowd moans. A reporter comments, "They felt they had been cheated. He didn't jump after
all."

In Nazi Germany a tyrannical government gradually took
control. The people accepted Hitler. He promised them jobs. The
store windows of Jewish-owned businesses were smashed. The
people were indifferent, or secretly rejoiced. "So what if the
storm troopers scared a few Jews. They deserved it." Soon an
entire nation was mobilized for war. The industrialists who supported the little signpainter had become his captive. The German
said, "It cannot happen here." The German Jew said, "Hitler
cannot be serious. We are good Germans. We are law-abiding
citizens. This is our country." The population was unconcerned.
Then came concentration camps and death. Six million Jews
died. Remaining silent is also an act that can be moral or immoral.

A Just Society

A moral person actively seeks to fashion a more just society.
He is not indifferent. In his own community, he is not afraid
to get involved in controversial issues. If a group of parents raises
unjust objections to sex education, he goes to a school-board
meeting to present the student's point of view. If a teacher is
victimized unfairly by a young girl who claims foul play (which
has occurred from time to time), he is not afraid to testify as a
character witness for the accused teacher.

If you see a situation that demands action, you should not
be silent. A young girl is struck by a car on her way to school.
She and her friends cross a dangerous highway with no traffic
light. You circulate a petition to have a light installed. You discover that the local state assemblyman is willing to plead your
case. We forget that the essence of democracy is the right of

peaceful petition. Lawmakers want to know what is important to you. They are elected to serve the people. But they must be told what the people want and need.

A Negro family moves into your neighborhood. False stories are circulated about them. You walk over and say hello. You help to make them feel welcome. You help to set an example of neighborliness. Soon you will find that others will follow your example. The new family will win acceptance. You did not stand idly by. You were not a critic. You stepped forward to help.

After much thought and careful study, you decide to organize a political club in your town. You persuade other young people to join you. At meetings in your home, you invite candidates for office to speak to your group. You become informed. Soon you are passing out leaflets and ringing doorbells. You become involved in making democracy work. You are busy doing something truly worthwhile. It does not take long to discover that local candidates are eager for an audience. In a few years you and your friends will be registered voters. You do influence your parents, even if you are not old enough to vote. The candidate who believes 18-year-olds should vote will win enthusiastic support from youth—provided he has other worthwhile ideas and programs. When you reach voting age you will be able to make intelligent choices. Having listened to candidates and worked for them, you will be able to distinguish the honest from the dishonest politician. Democracy will no longer be abstract. Unlike so many adults, you will not stay away from the polls on Election Day, or have to search frantically before going to the polling place for information on the candidates. You will know for whom to cast your ballot because you have been involved in the political process.

A just society is not a gift from heaven. Men must work to make it so. Minority children are bused into your school. Fear and suspicion arise that they will disrupt classes. You discover that they are more scared of you than you are of them. You extend the hand of friendship. Soon the school is integrated. When false rumors of trouble are circulated, you do not listen. You seek to obtain the facts. Instead of riots, there is peace. You have an open mind. You do not panic because a new situation arises.

The newspaper speaks of starving children in Biafra. You contact the Biafran Relief Society to find out how you can help. Soon you are ringing doorbells, to raise money to feed the starving children. You do more than just say, "Isn't it a shame," or, "Someone ought to do something." You actually do something to help. You get involved. Your act is moral—and also satisfying. Deep satisfaction is to be had in helping someone else. The young have moral concerns. Youth cares.

You have strong feelings about American foreign policy. Before you act, you read up on everything you can find. You carefully study what has happened in the past. You write to the State Department for material about our American policy abroad. You invite politicians of differing viewpoints to speak before a group of your friends. After much debate and discussion, you reach a conclusion. It may be that you will decide to support our government on a certain issue. Or you may feel that our government is wrong. As a thinking person you make your feelings known. You write letters. You discuss the matter. You may decide to take part in a prayer peace vigil. Or you may come to the conclusion that the executive branch of our government is right and should be supported. You think, discuss, study—and then act. You do not join a peace march just to meet boys or girls. If you do march for peace it is because you are convinced the cause is right.

You feel that youth should have a greater voice in the affairs of your church or synagogue. So you ask to have the right to present your ideas to the Board. Soon you may find that you are welcome to participate in adult deliberations on church or synagogue policy. The National Institutions of Reform Judaism have urged the individual congregations to appoint concerned young people as voting members of congregational boards of trustees. At the national biennial gathering of Reform Judaism, the young people spoke and voted on the major resolutions. Instead of saying, "The church or synagogue does not care about me," it is better to seek greater personal involvement. Youth is welcome in most religious movements. If religion is to have a future, the young people must have a voice in shaping it.

In the congregation I serve, the students in our religious school are consulted when curriculum revision takes place. Religious leaders are eager to know what will attract and inspire today's youth. If religion is a bore to youth, then changes are very much in order.

Tolerance of Other Opinions

The young accuse adults of not listening. Sometimes young people will not listen to adults—or even to other young people. On college campuses shouting matches have taken place. No one listens to the opposition. "I'm right and you're wrong." That is a form of totalitarianism. A totalitarian feels he has the total or whole truth—and nothing but the truth. He has worked out the answers, and whatever you say will matter little.

The word "tolerance" irks many individuals. They feel it implies condescension. "I will tolerate you, but I will not accept you." When used in that sense, it certainly is irksome. Still we must be tolerant of those who disagree with us. They have a right to their opinion. It may be far from the truth. Yet, to deny them the voice to speak is a form of immorality. So long as a man does not incite to violence and death (for example, crying "Fire!" in a crowded theater when there is no fire), that person has a right to be heard. When students invite a guest speaker to a campus, that person should be listened to, without booing and catcalls. He may not represent what you feel is the truth. Still, he has the right to speak. You have the obligation to extend him common courtesy.

Family life becomes more tolerable and pleasant when we show respect for those in our homes. You have a right to expect your parents to listen to your ideas. Conversely, they have a right to expect you to listen to them. Discussion is a two-way street.

"I Never Hurt Anyone"

In popular parlance, we hear the phrase, "He is a good person. He never hurt anyone in his life." It may be true. But he may never have helped anyone, either. Not to hurt others is a beginning of morality. Yet a moral person may be forced to inflict hurt on others. He may have to exert authority. He may have to restrain a man about to commit a crime. A policeman acts in a moral way when he defends the innocent. The criminal may be injured in the process.

Morality is not passive. It means little just to stand aside when injustice runs rampant. For most of us, the beginning of morality is not to injure others. Live and let live is part of our approach to problems. However, we must go one step beyond that passive approach. A recluse never hurts anyone. He lives to himself. He shuts himself off from the outside world. He does not get involved. He is not the model to follow. To live means to be involved with one's fellow human beings. "He would never hurt a fly." Suppose the fly is a carrier of disease? It may be the act of greater morality to kill the fly, before it brings death to others.

The moral person does not seek to hurt his fellow man. He is aware of the ego of the next person. Yet always to remain silent can be a disservice. "I just couldn't bring myself to tell him where he is making a mistake." How often we hear those words! The true friend is the only one who can be honest with you. You will accept criticism from her, because you know she is sincere. It may hurt to hear the unpleasant words. In the long run, it can be very helpful. TV commercials speak of a mouthwash to stop bad breath. The commercial says, "Even her best friend wouldn't tell her." A best friend *should* tell her—as tactfully as possible.

"All Men Are My Brothers"

Religion teaches "Thou shalt love thy neighbor as thyself." In other words, one must care as much about his neighbor as he cares about himself. Some psychologists say that we must love ourselves properly before we can show respect and affection for others. From self-love we move to the realm of love for those near us.

A moral person can truly say he believes in the brotherhood of man. If every man is my brother, then any man who suffers is important. When he is in pain, I also am in pain. In practical terms, we cannot live in a constant state of suffering. At any given moment, millions are living in hunger, despair, and sickness. What can we do? Some say, "The problems are too great. There is no point in doing anything." A better answer might be, "I shall select one small area where I can do some good. There is a tutorial program in the slum-ghetto of our town. I can offer my services to help teach the disadvantaged to read." Such an act does not make the newspaper headlines. Yet, after all the marches and speeches, the difficult tasks remain—some are sheer drudgery—that still must be accomplished. A teenager gives a few hours a week to help out—without pay—in a youth center in the so-called "bad" part of town. He may never see his picture in the newspaper or on the TV screen. But he has the inner satisfaction of knowing he has done something to improve the human condition.

Crimes Against Yourself?

The waste of one's talent has been called an immoral act. Many have great potential. They score well on aptitude tests. They have the brains and the ability to achieve, but they waste away their days. Countless doctors, nurses, lawyers, business executives, and engineers have never entered their fields. Why? Somewhere along the way, they have "dropped out." The person who is on a perpetual vacation—unless he is a philosopher seeking some great inner truth—contributes nothing to mankind.

Morality becomes the issue. A young man is a premedical student in college. He has talent and ability. Then, during his senior year, he drops out of school. He decides to spend all of his

time on a surfboard. He feels he is "fulfilling" himself. He is out
of the rat race. He says, "There are many others studying medicine. Let them become the rich doctors. I want to do my thing
on a surfboard." Has this young man done something immoral?
Is it a crime to deny society the services of a future doctor? Some
would argue that a young man with such an attitude should not
be given a medical education, since at some point he would drop
out. They would say, "Let us educate people for jobs they really
want, and for roles they truly wish to fill." What do you think
about this? Is there a moral obligation to develop one's talents,
skills, and abilities to the greatest extent possible, even if you
suddenly decide you do not wish to do so? How free should a
man be? Should he be free as a bird—to do what he wishes—
or does he have obligations to society?

A young man enters the office of the public school principal.
"Under no conditions will I follow this dress code." The principal
explains that a committee is studying the matter, and newer,
more liberal regulations will be forthcoming in a few weeks. He
says, "I demand an answer now. You cannot tell me how to dress.
What I learn is important. How I score on tests is important.
How I dress, or the length of my hair, is unimportant." The
young man may be right. But he is impatient. He will not submit
to any authority. He drops out of school, to "show them." Whom
does he hurt? The principal? His fellow students? No, he is hurting only himself. Someone has said, "A person is his own worst
enemy." It is usually true. The man who complains he is always
down on his luck is making excuses. Most of the time we make
our own luck—be it good or bad.

Is There a New Morality?

I do not believe that there really is a "new" morality. What
we see today is a "different" morality. The difference is that
today's youth believes in greater freedom and less censorship.
The new morality advocates speak of the open society in which
each can do his thing so long as it does not hurt someone else.

We see today both a rebellion against authority, and at the same time a desire to share in forming new authority patterns. The congregation where I serve as Rabbi has instituted a program whereby young people are invited to attend all adult committee meetings. The young can come to any adult decision-making gathering. They are recognized, and they are heard. They can speak, petition, state, and propose new ideas. They are fully a part of the life of the congregation. They were not given such privileges overnight. Much thought was given by the adult leadership. The pros and cons were debated over many months and even years. But the step was taken. The effects have been gratifying.

The new morality is different in that our youth-oriented society is more responsive than it has ever been to the yearnings of young people. The voices of the young finally turned many adults against the war in Vietnam. The demand for action to eradicate slums, poverty, and disease have been voiced by the young, who are not afraid. One Negro woman remarked, "My generation was willing to accept whatever little we were given. My approach did not work. Now I am learning from my own child. She is making demands upon society. She is teaching me what I must do." Yes, there is a turnabout. The young are teaching their parents. The reins of leadership are more and more shared. Not only does youth speak out; the adults listen to what you are saying.

Adults are not ready to accept everything that you declare as valid. Free love without responsibility is seldom popular with parents. They have learned that sex without affection and commitment contains seeds of danger and difficulty. Film stars may live together without being married, but such individuals are not yet the models of conduct for society. Moreover, when the first child is born, such common-law arrangements are usually solemnized by the clergy. You will have to make certain decisions about the morality of sexual behavior. Despite our oversexed society and the open offerings of films rated "x," the actual conduct of young persons may not be drastically different today from what it was many years ago. Certainly there is more permissiveness. Yet the young are not all of one mind about discarding all codes of sexual conduct. Surprisingly enough, a large number of them have serious doubts about the new sexual freedom. The so-called single standard is all right for others, but—say many young men—I would still like the girl I marry to be a virgin, or if not a virgin, I would like to *believe* she is chaste.

If youth is truly open-minded, then all authority systems have to be examined. You may discover that you really need guidance —and someone to set some limits of conduct. On a TV panel show, a group of young people told of how they finally were able to escape from drug addiction. A young girl said, "I used to lie to my parents. I told them I was going to a hospital for help. Actually, I was just getting in deeper and deeper. Finally, my father was smart enough to personally take me to a drug addiction center. This started me on the way back to a normal life. Without the help of my dad, I would have been lost."

Areas exist in which the adult society can say, "You must." In matters affecting safety (traffic laws) and health (proper medical care), you may find that unquestioning obedience is demanded. Beyond safety and health lies a wide area of free choice. However, parents can say "no" when your actions adversely affect others in the family, for example, when you have a fight with a brother or sister. When you are young, you have the "voice" but parents often determine the "vote." You may not be thrilled if your father changes jobs and you have to move to another community. Still, in most cases you must move with your family— even though the decision is unpleasant or distressing. As long as you are a minor, you will lack full and complete freedom. For example, if you are below a certain age, you cannot get married without your parents' consent. In most states you cannot vote at age 18. Adult society makes the laws. In three states (Hawaii, Louisiana, New York) you can drink before you are 21. Elsewhere, you cannot. You may feel such laws are foolish; maybe they are. But until they are changed, adult society demands that you obey them. You will argue, "I can be drafted at 19, but cannot vote until I'm 21." Laws are not always consistent. As you grow older, you will have more of a voice in altering them.

As a minister, I counsel a steady stream of people who come to my study. They arrive from all walks of life. Those who have lived the life of complete freedom are often the ones who are most deeply troubled. The new morality is no guarantor of happiness. Before making a choice for the new way—especially in the new sex ethic—give the matter careful thought. To be civilized means to have some standards. A world of complete freedom can spell complete chaos.

A Final Word

This book has sought to give a sociological approach to the new morality. I have tried to direct my thoughts to the current problems of your world—and your life. You will be the final arbiter. After all is said and done, you will react to this changing world—and to its changing moral standards—as you see fit.

I do feel that you should have my own opinion on the new morality. I believe much that is positive and good is to be found in the new morality—when we use the term to imply the new openness of discussion on all issues—war, sex, violence, the Pill, drugs, and the meaning of life. For the first time, parents are willing to meet their children more than half way on the great personal and social issues of our times.

I feel that the new standards are part of a two-way dialogue. Parents are listening. Teenagers should also listen. Something is to be said for experience. It may not be the greatest teacher, but experience gives one a history of what has happened to others. You feel that your times are different. They *are* different. Each age is somewhat unlike the age that has gone before it. My generation grew up in the Depression, and lived through World War II and the Korean conflict. Yours is the generation of Vietnam and the Pill. Yours is the age of student protest. Yours is the age in which youth has found its voice. Yours is the concerned generation. You have made your parents ill at ease in this affluent society. Your new morality demands an honest appraisal of priorities. You have asked us, "Why land men on the moon when men on earth live in hovels and are starving?" You have said that swollen bellies in Biafra should not exist alongside huge sums spent to build ABM missiles. Your generation is largely pacifistic. You cannot justify war—in any form. Even wars of defense take on a strange meaning when you consider them. The words of Isaiah—calling upon men to "beat their swords into plowshares"—this is the thrust of your age.

You wish freedom and independence—in thought, dress, and action. You want to do your thing, and want everyone else to have the right to do his thing—so long as no one gets hurt in the process. You fear no one—and no person. Your heroes are the peacemakers. The warriors do not delight you. The ranks of R.O.T.C. on campuses have diminished. Even the athletic heroes carry less weight with your generation. You are individualists and nonconformists. Why? Because there are few patterns with which to conform. Organized religion becomes less organized. Coffee-house priests and rabbis join you in common causes. Most of you would endorse nonviolent protest. You see nothing wrong in breaking an unjust law. In fact, for you to do so is to act in a moral way. With the Biblical prophet Amos you would say, "I take no delight in your feasts or solemn assemblies . . . but let justice run down like waters, and righteousness like a mighty stream. Seek good, that you may live, and so the Lord God of hosts shall be with you."

You are willing to examine the teachings of all religions. Many of you belong to a particular church or synagogue. Yet you may have many doubts about the value of organized religion. You listen to the clergymen. You wish religion to speak out against the evils of the day. Yet you want the freedom to define what is evil and what is good.

For many of your generation, man is the measure of all things. Many of you are humanistic. You feel that man is doing his thing, with little guidance from anyone other than his own intuitive feelings. You rely on intuition and experience—and the opinions of others—to help you reach decisions and make choices.

You respect the gifts of science. You are fearful when science makes bombs instead of rebuilding cities. Sex is a private matter. War is a public affair. Private matters should be left to the individual. Public matters—such as war or peace—are items high on the agenda because they involve survival. Unless man survives war, he cannot enjoy happiness and fulfillment—and love.

You do not trust those who speak of more armaments for defense. You equate defense with war. Few conflicts are ever justified—in your eyes. You do not opt for complete nonviolence. But I feel that you are coming very close to a Gandhi-like approach. You wish to live and let live. You follow the teachings of Rabbi Hillel who said, "Do not do unto others as you would not have them do unto you." Let others live. Do not hurt them. Yet you want men to "love thy neighbor as thyself." You see love as the ultimate solution to the ills of society. Love leads to peace —and the end of conflict. You feel our society fosters competition —so you would like to see grades abolished (many of you feel this way). You envision a society in which each person can fulfill himself, without competing or hurting his fellow man. You will fight for such a world—hopefully in a nonviolent way. You will march—as you did on Vietnam Moratorium Day—October 15, 1969—because a nonviolent march expresses your mood. Some 250,000 of you marched in Washington one month later. You will work for those who believe in peace. To do so is moral. At times you may be used by enemies of our country. You are willing to take that chance, if it will effect proper change. You may find yourself with strange and sinister allies in your quest for peace. You are not deterred, if you believe the cause is right.

Your moral standards go beyond freedom from dress and style codes. It is more than long hair versus short hair, or straight kids versus hip kids. It is a matter of mood. Yours is a mood of restlessness and impatience. You will examine the old codes, even as you look for new ones. If the new morality and the new freedom do not work, you may look for some sort of authoritarianism. In your quest for freedom, you must be careful not to deny freedom to those who disagree with you. Your inclinations are good. They are highly moral. To the adult world, you look confused. When your parents were young, their parents felt they were wrong. You are not reared in the age of obedience. You have been given increasingly larger doses of freedom by your parents. You have been consulted. Seldom have you been disciplined. For better or for worse, you have been raised in the age of psychology, in which each is expected to develop to the fullest.

You are not overly grateful to the older generation. You believe that you could have done things a lot better. You criticize. You are not willing to forgive your parents for their mistakes. You are harsh on all established institutions—religion, government, business, industry. You subject one and all—and yourself —to the new morality. It is a morality that demands openness of mind, mouth, and heart. It speaks of an honesty in human relationships. It does not place sex on a pedestal as something special. It looks askance at Puritan sexual ethics and codes. It says, "The old ways did not work. We have wars, mental breakdowns, divorces, pot, the Pill—and unhappiness. Maybe a new morality is the answer. It cannot be any worse than what we have now."

Your words at times sound radical and far-out. In actual practice you often reflect the ideas, values, and attitudes of your parents. You are often shocked and outraged at the same things. Sometimes you are even more shocked. The difference between your generation and ours is that your generation will have to fight the wars and live longer in the pollution—and continue to confront the new challenge of space-age technology and its values. You are in the postindustrial new age of scientific computers and rapid change, in which values have been sloughed off with great rapidity. Shifting sands offer little ground or place to take a stand. Some of you have found your values in your church or synagogue. Others have discovered a meaning for life in working for causes. Still others will seek truth in patriotism and unquestioning faith in the country and its leadership.

Your new morality is openness and honesty and living life to its fullest—without rushing to acquire things. Big banquets tend to turn you off. A guitar in a coffee house will turn you on. Comforts are wanted. But, even more, you want something in which to believe. Your new god (with a small "g") is the new morality that speaks of a continuous search. The answers are not yet discovered. The life-style is ever changing.

Bob Dylan has captured the restless spirit of today's youth, as he issues a warning to parents in the song, "The Times They Are A-Changin'." He sings:

> Come gather 'round, people, wherever you roam
> And admit that the waters around you have grown,
> And accept it that soon you'll be drenched to the bone.
> If your time to you is worth savin'
> Then you'd better start swimmin' or you'll sink like a stone,
> For the times they are a-changin'.
>
> Come mothers and fathers throughout the land
> And don't criticize what you can't understand;
> Your sons and your daughters are beyond your command;
> Your old road is rapidly agin'.
> Please get out of the new one if you can't lend your hand
> For the times are rapidly changin'."

It is true that "the waters have grown." Parents and children must swim together if relationships are "worth savin'." As you grow up, you begin to move beyond the command of your parents. The old ways are "rapidly agin'." But not everything new is good, nor is everything old necessarily bad. Consider carefully before you act. Do you wish to discard the old morality? Give it another look. Within a few years, the new morality may become old-fashioned. Perhaps "mini"-morals will give way to "maxi"-morals at some future date. Few things in life are constant. An ancient Hebrew prophet tried to decide what God required of man. His answer: "Do justly, love mercy, walk humbly." A just society is one fashioned with mercy and humility. Care deeply. Think carefully. Act out of a sense of justice, honesty, and decency. Another sage said, "Why were only Adam and Eve created at the beginning of the world—and not additional couples? To show that each and every person—as an *individual*—is important." You *do* count. What you do, how you think—and the way you act—does make a difference. *You* matter!

APPENDIX A

Thought Questions

CHAPTER I:
1. How constant is the search for morality?
2. Does anyone care—really—about morality?
3. How important is the home in shaping moral values?
4. Would the ideal family be a bore?
5. Are maturity and morality related in any way?

CHAPTER II:
1. Do we need heroes?
2. What is the danger of hero worship?
3. Are teachers usually fair?
4. How accurate are the student comments about teachers—as noted in this chapter?
5. Who is to blame for cheating? The student? The teacher? Both?
6. Can youth really influence a school board?
7. Can authority figures in a school still command respect?
8. Do you feel it is immoral to be treated as a number and not as a person? Why, or why not?
9. Is too much fuss being made over the lack of personalization in society?
10. Must you be treated as an individual to know that you truly matter?
11. How real is the generation gap?
12. How closely should the generations communicate?
13. When does communication become "nosy"?
14. Does technology reduce man to a number? Must technology always make us less important—and less useful?
15. Is science immoral when it lessens the dignity and worth of a person?

162

16. Does affluence lead to immorality? Why? Why not?
17. What is good about affluence?
18. Does affluence make us less human?

CHAPTER III:

1. Is there a way for a parent to exert authority in the matter of the sexual behavior of a teenager?
2. Is it ever desirable for parents to set limits to such behavior?
3. What is good about sex education in the schools?
4. Do you feel your school should have more intensive sex education?
5. What areas of sex education should be stressed by the schools?
6. Should the schools teach moral values as part of a sex education program?
7. Are there any dangers in sex education in the schools?
8. How should a wise parent impart sexual knowledge to a child?
9. Why are sex and love often considered to be the same thing? Should they be?
10. Is sex always a private matter? Can sex hurt others? How?
11. Should an unwed mother care about what her friends think or say?
12. Do adults make too much of a fuss over premarital sex? Is it ever morally justified?
13. What do you think of situational ethics?
14. What is good about romantic love? What are its faults?
15. How do you feel about the double standard?

CHAPTER IV:

1. Is sexual morality changing, or merely different?
2. Should the clergy be firmer in counseling young people as to sexual standards of behavior?
3. Can a clergyman be effective in guiding young people if he is noncensorious? Must he always be comforting and understanding?
4. How much should religion have to say in shaping our sexual morality?
5. Is God the ultimate source and judge of sexual morality?

6. Are sociology and psychology helpful in aiding us to understand and evaluate our conduct? Do they exert undue influence? Do they lead to undue permissiveness?
7. Should our actions be governed by what most people are doing?
8. Can anyone really make an independent decision?
9. Do we need public forums at which youth and adults can discuss and debate the issue of sexual conduct?
10. How helpful are the experts in sex education?
11. Does the fear element (pregnancy, venereal disease, social criticism, etc.) affect sexual behavior in any significant way?
12. Should mothers encourage their unwed daughters to take the Pill? Would such encouragement tend to make a girl act more freely in sexual matters?
13. Someone said, "To give your daughter the Pill is like handing a loaded gun to a small child." How do you react to that statement?
14. Should colleges act *in loco parentis?* Is education the sole function of a college? Should they be involved in sexual conduct? Should college dorms have limits on visiting hours?
15. Is sex a microethical issue or a macroethical concern?
16. Have young people stopped moralizing over sexual conduct? Can a girl still get a reputation as being "fast"?
17. What's good about the dating game? Or is it foolish?
18. Are we being drowned in a sea of permissiveness?
19. Why is there a gap between society's standards and actual sexual conduct? Can the gap be closed?
20. Must you follow the crowd in sexual conduct? Can you evolve your own code of behavior? How?

CHAPTER V:

1. Is TV "alive," as McLuhan holds? Is the medium the message that massages us—too much?
2. Why do we permit the media to shape our attitudes—or do we?
3. Which comes first—our attitudes, or the shaping of them by the media?
4. Have you ever had an "I—Thou" relationship? Is all life meeting?
5. What's wrong with a credit-card society? Should companies be prevented from sending unsolicited credit cards through the mail?
6. Is frugality dead?

7. Can the media be employed to help society? How?
8. How immoral is advertising?
9. Does TV report news, or create it?
10. Should TV be censored? Is censorship of the media a moral issue? Why? Why not?
11. Do films significantly influence sexual standards and behavior?
12. Should films be "rated"?
13. Does violence in the media stimulate viewers to criminal acts?
14. Should youth be allowed to read and see everything? Should all laws controlling pornography be suspended?
15. To what extent are the young exploited by the media?
16. Is the moral direction of the media largely in your hands?

CHAPTER VI:

1. Is pot the first step to hard drugs?
2. Is marijuana harmful or harmless? Why do you think it is, or is not, dangerous?
3. Do drug raids do more harm than good? Why? Why not?
4. Are penalties for drug use too harsh? Why? Why not?
5. Should pot be legalized? Why? Why not?
6. Why has pot use spread to all levels of society?
7. Did the Linkletter LSD tragedy influence your attitude on mind-expanding drugs? Why? Why not?
8. Can we stop the spread of hard drug use? How? Who is to blame for narcotics traffic—the manufacturer, the pusher, or the user?
9. How much good can a place like Topic House really do?
10. Is drug use immoral? Why? Why not? Does it affect society? How?
11. Why do the innocent suffer when the family has a drug-addicted member? What should the family do? Is it ever moral to turn your own child over to the law if he is on drugs?
12. Do drug users become heroes at your school? Why? Why not?

CHAPTER VII:

1. Is hypocrisy the main complaint of youth against the adult world? Why? Why not?

2. Must a person always practice what he preaches?
3. Why does this new age say that respect must be earned? Was it not always true that respect had to be earned?
4. Are adults overly concerned about doing things for appearances' sake? Is such concern ever necessary?
5. Should we have landed a man on the moon while starvation and war go on here on the earth? Is this part of our moral problem?
6. How immoral is the industrial-military complex? Does it exist, or is it just a term?
7. What is immoral about some white attitudes toward blacks?
8. Do blacks often overreact in evaluating the white man?
9. Can we build a moral society, based on true brotherhood and peace? How? What can you do to bring this about?
10. Is an integrated society a desirable moral goal—in all cases? What of the blacks who demand a separate black state in America?
11. Do black-studies programs lead to greater separation between the races?
12. Will blacks ever fully trust whites?
13. Are all wars immoral?
14. Is our country more moral than the enemy in wartime?
15. Is there such a thing as a just war?
16. Should an entire nation be held accountable for the crimes of its leaders in wartime? Why? Why not?
17. Does guilt have its limits? How long should the Germans feel guilty over Hitler's barbaric acts?
18. Did the events at My Lai hamlet seriously damage American moral standing?
19. Is the Vietnamese war immoral? What of those who say we are preserving the democratic government of South Vietnam?
20. How moral is it for the government to appeal to the so-called silent majority for support?
21. What is honesty? Why are some honest whereas others are not? Who is to blame? Parents? Teachers? Friends? Our society?
22. Is it moral to disobey an unjust law? What are the limits of dissent?
23. Is there anything left in which you can still believe?
24. Is the work ethic of America about to be discarded?

25. How important is work? Do adults place too much stress on the job—and the status of a job?
26. How important is security? Do you view security differently from your parents?
27. Must we destroy society first so as to build a new world?
28. How can peaceful change be achieved?
29. What can youth learn from adults? Can you profit from your parents' mistakes? Can you learn from their achievements?

CHAPTER VIII:

1. Should we consider the problems of the future when making moral decisions today? Do you owe something to future generations? What?
2. How important is it to think before you act? Must thought precede action? Why?
3. When is silence or inaction immoral?
4. What can you do—in a positive way—to be helpful to society?
5. Do the young think too much of themselves—and not enough of others? Is youth overly self-centered?
6. How can you share in adult decision-making?
7. Does every opinion have the right to be heard? What about stifling the voices of those who advocate the violent overthrow of our government? Should they be silenced?
8. What can religious institutions do to involve the youth in their programs?
9. Can religion reassert itself as a powerful moral force?
10. What do we mean by crimes against oneself? Should we force a person to stop wasting his talents and skills?
11. Should a person have complete freedom as to his life-style, even if society needs his talents? Is this a moral issue?
12. How can parents and children work together to attain a happier home life? What should parents do? What should children do?
13. How new is the new morality? Is it a throwback to paganism? Or does it show a new willingness to examine all facets of life in complete honesty?
14. Can we ever have a society in which no man will hurt his neighbor?

15. Will the new morality give way to an even newer morality, as yet unknown?

16. Is the old morality dead—or just waiting to come back into style in another age?

Footnotes

1. *Life* magazine, Vol. LXVII, July 18, 1969.
2. Ibid., p. 19.
3. Ibid., p. 21.
4. Thelma C. Purtell, *The Intelligent Parents' Guide to Teen-Agers.* Paul S. Erikson, Inc., New York, 1961, p. 3.
5. *Life* magazine, June 13, 1969, p. 37.
6. Ibid., p. 52.
7. *Life* magazine, May 16, 1969, p. 24.
8. Ibid., p. 25.
9. "The Harris Survey." *Long Island Press,* July 3, 1969.
10. Ibid.
11. "Class of '69: The Violent Years." *Newsweek,* June 23, 1969, p. 70.
12. Ibid., p. 68.
13. Jerry L. Avorn, *Up Against the Ivy Wall.* Atheneum, New York, 1969, p. 33.
14. *New York Times,* May 20, 1969, p. 49.
15. News release, April 22, 1969, from State Education Department, reprint by Wantagh High School, pp. 1, 2.
16. Sex Education Program, 7th and 8th Grade Report to the Board of Education, March 1969, Wantagh Public Schools, p. 3.
17. Ibid., p. 4.
18. W. H. R. Rivers, *The Todas.* New York, The Macmillan Co., 1906, pp. 515 ff.
19. Raoul de Roussy de Sales, "Love in America." *The Atlantic,* May 1938, p. 645.
20. Willard Waller and Reuben Hill, *The Family: A Dynamic Interpretation* (New York, Holt, Rinehart & Winston, Inc., 1951) pp. 155–56. As quoted in *Sociology, A Systematic Approach,* by James W. Vander Zanden. The Ronald Press Co., New York, p. 327.
21. James W. Vander Zanden, *Sociology, A Systematic Approach.* The Ronald Press Co., New York, 1965, p. 330.
22. Interfaith Statement on Sex Education by the National Council of Churches, Commission on Marriage and Family; Synagogue Council

of America, Committee on Family; United States Catholic Conference, Family Life Bureau, June 8, 1968.
23. Ibid.
24. Ibid.
25. Ibid.
26. Quotations from Alfred Kinsey's *Sexual Behavior in the Human Female* and Winston Ehrmann's *Premarital Dating Behavior*, as found in James W. Vander Zanden, *Sociology, A Systematic Approach*. Ronald Press Company, New York, 1965, page 340.
27. Ernest W. Burgess and Paul Wallin, *Engagement and Marriage*. Philadelphia, J. B. Lippincott Co., 1953, pp. 332–333.
28. Gerald R. Leslie, *The Family in Social Context*. Oxford University Press, New York, London, Toronto, 1967, p. 418.
29. *Medical Economics*, November 28, 1966, pp. 277–278.
30. Ibid., p. 278.
31. "A Schoolman's Guide to Marshall McLuhan." John M. Culkin, S. J., *Saturday Review*, March 18, 1967, p. 51.

Bibliography

Avorn, Jerry L., *Up Against the Ivy Wall*. New York, Atheneum, 1969.

Burgess, Ernest W., and Wallin, Paul, *Engagement and Marriage*. Philadelphia, J. B. Lippincott Co., 1953.

De Sales, Raoul de Roussy, "Love in America." *The Atlantic,* May, 1938.

Interfaith Statement on Sex Education by the National Council of Churches, Commission on Marriage and Family; Synagogue Council of America, Committee on Family; United States Catholic Conference, Family Life Bureau, June 8, 1968.

Leslie, Gerald R., *The Family in Social Context*. New York, Oxford University Press, London, Toronto, 1967.

Life magazine, May 16, 1969.

Life magazine, June 13, 1969.

Life magazine, July 18, 1969.

Long Island Press, "The Harris Survey," July 3, 1969.

Mandelbaum, Bernard, *Choose Life*. New York, Random House, 1968. Quotation from the Midrash.

Medical Economics, November 28, 1966.

News Release, April 22, 1969, from State Education Department reprint by Wantagh High School.

Newsweek, "Class of '69: The Violent Years," June 23, 1969.

New York Times, May 20, 1969.

Purtell, Thelma C., *The Intelligent Parents' Guide to Teen-Agers*. New York, Paul S. Erikson, Inc., 1961.

Quotations from Alfred Kinsey's *Sexual Behavior in the Human Female* and Winston Ehrmann's *Premarital Dating Behavior,*

171

as found in James W. Vander Zanden, *Sociology, A Systematic Approach*. New York, Ronald Press Company, 1965.

Rivers, W. H. R., *The Todas*. New York, the Macmillan Co., 1906.

Sex Education Program, 7th and 8th Grade Report to the Board of Education, March 1969, Wantagh Public Schools.

Vander Zanden, James W., *Sociology, A Systematic Approach*. New York, Ronald Press Company, 1965.

Waller, Willard and Hill, Reuben, *The Family: A Dynamic Interpretation*. New York, Holt, Rinehart & Winston, Inc., 1951. As quoted in *Sociology, A Systematic Approach*, by James W. Vander Zanden. New York, Ronald Press Company.

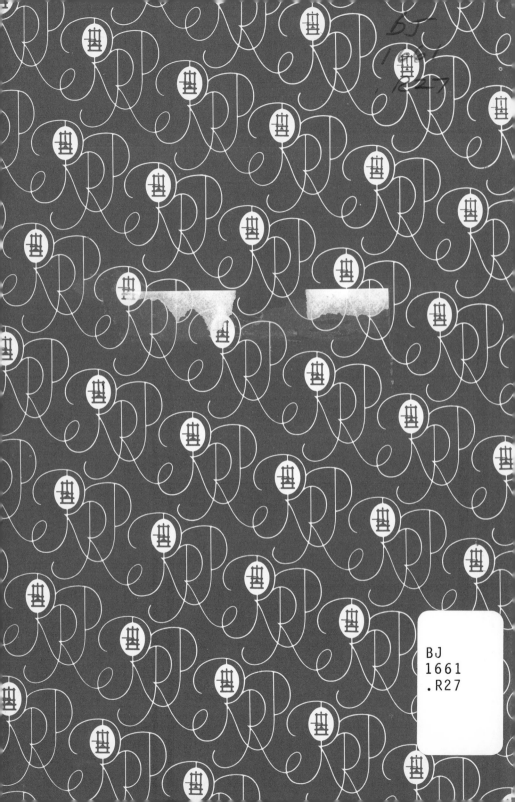